COLLINS

The 500 Best
GARDEN
PLANTS

COLLINS

The 500 Best GARDEN PLANTS

PATRICK TAYLOR

HarperCollins*Publishers*

First published in 1993
Reprinted in 2000 by
HarperCollins*Publishers* Ltd
77–85 Fulham Palace Road, London W6 8JB

This book was devised and produced by
Open Books Publishing Ltd, Willow Cottage
Cudworth, near Ilminster TA19 0PS, Somerset, UK

Designer: Andrew Barron,
Andrew Barron and Collis Clements Associates

A CIP catalogue record for this book is available from
the British Library

ISBN: 0-00-710381-6

Printed in China

CONTENTS

———— ❧ ————

INTRODUCTION

& ACKNOWLEDGEMENTS

I have chosen the plants described in this book because I like them and I have tried to explain why I think them good. In my visits to literally hundreds of gardens, doing research for books or just for fun, and in countless conversations with gardeners, I began to notice that certain excellent plants appeared again and again in gardens that I especially liked. This is a personal selection but certain rules have governed it. As far as possible the plants have qualities in addition to merely dazzling flowers. In a small or modestly sized garden, space cannot be given to some substantial shrub whose only virtue is to produce wonderful flowers for a couple of weeks in the year. So I have paid attention to the merits of foliage, habit, bark, berries, buds and scent – to all those attributes which contribute to the garden-worthiness of a distinguished plant. I have also where possible chosen species or old cultivars that have proved their worth. Each year new cultivars pour out from the nurseries but only rarely do they add to the essential repertory of garden plants. This does not mean, however, that I include examples of all the older groups of plants. I cannot, for example, find a species of forsythia that I would regard as a top garden plant. Some plants, such as heathers, while admirable for clothing remote highland landscapes, seem to me extremely difficult to use harmoniously in conjunction with other garden plants.

On the whole I have selected plants that have no especially elaborate cultivation needs. However, it is a myth that any good garden can be 'maintenance free', and in the same way plants that are 'cultivation free' are very often weeds. Gardening is not an occupation for lazy people and all the best gardens are, without exception, the product of hard work and much careful thought. In such gardens it is not merely planting and cultivation skills that are evident but also expert pruning and training.

In the case of especially large genera – for example rhododendrons and roses – I have only hinted at the possibilities. There are few gardens which have the climate and space to do justice to the finest rhododendrons. If you *do* have the perfect site for these marvellous plants you will need something much more elaborate than this book. Among the roses – a vast genus in terms of species and cultivars – I have picked a few which seem to me to illustrate their best virtues. But any gardener who becomes intensely interested in a particular group of plants will want to know more than I have room for and I include a list of specialist books on different groups of plants on pages 307–9.

The gardens that are most admired reveal a harmonious design in which a good range of beautiful plants are attractively disposed. Whereas larger gardens can afford to deploy seasonal plantings in different areas, smaller gardens, especially those overlooked by the windows of one's house, require a range of individual plants to show something of interest all year round. My own garden, in the middle of a town, is an eccentrically irregular rectangle 180ft/54m long by 45ft/12m wide. A large area is devoted to lawn which has been much used by my children for playing games. I am all too conscious that in a desire to have some attention-worthy plant always performing, and as a result of a fatal inability to resist a good plant, I have packed in too much heterogenous material at the expense of harmony. That is the perpetual dilemma of all keen gardeners with small gardens.

A hardiness rating is given for each plant, indicated by the letter Z and a numeral. Maps showing these zones in Europe and the USA are given on pages 310–11. The time of flowering I have indicated is applicable to the south of England, that is to say, roughly Zone 8. Readers living in milder or cooler areas will be able to adjust it according to their knowledge of local conditions. The maximum size given for each plant is what could be expected in a fairly protected garden in southern England.

Many nurseries and owners of private gardens have been generous with their help. I should especially like to thank the following: Avon Bulbs (particularly Joyce Hodgson, Chris Ireland-Jones and Alan Street); Bicton College; The Botanic Gardens, Bath; Broadleigh Gardens (Lady Skelmersdale); East Lambrook Manor (Andrew Norton); Hannays of Bath; Kingston Maurward College; Patricia Marrow (who has been endlessly kind); The National Trust for England and Wales (especially Diana Badham); The Royal Botanic Gardens, Kew (Jenny Evans); Westonbirt Arboretum.

The photographs were all taken by myself except for that on page 276 of *Catalpa bignonioïdes* which is by Andrew Lawson to whom I am most grateful.

My wife Caroline has edited my text with skill and patience; I would be more effusive but she is very strict about too many adjectives. Andrew Barron has designed the book and taken a valuable interest in it. My publishers, Pavilion Books, are a constant pleasure to deal with and I am in particular grateful to Helen Sudell and Colin Webb for their encouragement. In the USA Robert Conklin and Dale Johnson of Timber Press have given much friendly advice. Penelope Hobhouse has been a perpetual source of inspiration and deep knowledge; as was her late husband, John Malins, a marvellous gardener and the nicest of men, to whose memory I affectionately dedicate this book.

Patrick Taylor
Wells, Somerset

BULBS

Bulbs provide trouble-free ornamental planting over a very long season – indeed there is barely a month in the year without bulbs flowering in the garden. They give a dazzling display in late winter or spring when little else is in flower, and in that awkward season after the first burst of summer flowering in June, when interest can seem to flag, bulbs will produce some of the most splendid effects. Magnificent lilies in July, filling gaps left by earlier herbaceous plants, are followed by crinums, crocosmias and nerines. As summer turns into autumn small corners are enlivened by vivid little cyclamen and they in turn are followed by sternbergias which give way to snowdrops, aconites and crocuses and once again the whole explosion of spring bulbs.

Bulbs contribute much to the garden's most beautiful detail throughout the year. They also live harmoniously with other plants, occupying little space in the herbaceous border or among shrubs of whatever size. Many spring-flowering bulbs, for example, relish a moist position at flowering time under deciduous shrubs not yet in leaf, then enjoy the dry conditions that follow, as shrubs and herbaceous plants leaf up, before retreating underground until the following year.

Many bulbs – snowdrops, crocus, daffodils, for example – are easy to establish in self-perpetuating colonies, naturalizing happily without becoming excessively invasive. Others, like lilies and some tulips, are less easy to keep going, but immensely repay the trouble. Invaluable for smaller gardens, where they may be tucked into odd corners unsuitable for larger plants, bulbs provide brilliant fleeting ornament to the permanent, structural planting of gardens of any size.

I have included in this section, in addition to bulbs, corms, rhizomes and tubers which many gardeners and nurserymen commonly think of as bulbs.

Allium

A genus of over 700 species of the family Liliaceae/Alliaceae, widely distributed in the northern hemisphere. Like the culinary onion and garlic, all have a distinct onion-like scent when the leaves are crushed. The genus includes valuable and versatile garden plants but beware those that are dangerously invasive and may prove an embarrassment in the smaller garden.

Allium christophii
(*A. albopilosum*)
Origin: C. Asia, Iran, Turkey
Height: 30in/75cm
Z: 7

❧ This ornamental onion has one of the largest flower heads of any of its tribe. Between 6–10in/15–25cm across, it is smothered in June with an immense number of elegant star-shaped flowers, each 1½in/4cm across, its very narrow silvery violet petals set off by much darker anthers. In a densely planted border it will be supported by other plantings and the spherical flower heads will lie among other foliage like celestial footballs, looking especially beautiful among pale grey *Artemisia ludoviciana latiloba*. It will seed itself benignly and is equally at home in sun or part shade.

Allium karataviense
Origin: C. Asia
Height: 6in/15cm
Z: 8

❧ The leaves, which emerge in April, are the first sign of distinction in this allium. They are 6in/15cm long and generously wide, up to 4in/10cm, handsomely ribbed and curved and an attractive glaucous-green. The flower heads appear in May at the centre of the leaves and open into great spheres up to 4in/10cm across, of countless stars, very pale grey-violet in colour. The seed pods that follow are strikingly decorative, becoming a golden colour in the autumn. It needs a sunny site in light soil and may be propagated from the prolific seeds. It has a ghostly presence in the border. I have seen it very successfully planted among spreading *Geranium renardii*.

Allium moly
Origin: S.W. Europe
Height: 9in/22.5cm
Z: 7

❧ The foliage of this golden onion is grey-green, pointed and strap-like. The flowers in May or June are unlike any other onion: rich, dazzling yellow stars in upward-facing umbels. The colour is especially intense in semi-shade although it grows equally well in full sun. It likes a dry site and is excellent to grow massed at the feet of shrubs where it will relish the dry conditions.

Allium triquetrum

Allium triquetrum
Origin: S. Europe
Height: 6in/15cm
Z: 8

❧ In a shady corner in the garden this little allium has terrific character. It flowers in May, bearing several flowers on each fresh green stem, which is triangular in section. The flowers hang gracefully downwards, little white trumpets $^1/_2$in/1.25cm long, striped inside and out with thin green lines. It likes moist soil and flourishes in the shade. Grow it to follow hellebores and spring bulbs in a place of woodland character. It will seed itself with almost embarrassing abandon.

Alstroemeria

Alstroemeria Ligtu hybrids
Origin: Garden (Chile)
Height: 36in/90cm
Z: 6

There are about fifty species of alstroemeria, all tubers and rhizomes, in the family Liliaceae/ Alstroemeriaceae and native to South America.

❧ The leaves of this alstroemeria are a very decorative glaucous-green, slender and up to 5in/2cm long, carried on woody stems. The flowers in May or June are exotic and beautiful, open trumpet shapes, 2in/5cm long, varying in colour between pink and orange, with beautiful darker stripes inside the flowers. This is an admirable border plant, distinguished in flower and foliage. It needs rich soil and shows its flower colour best in a position of semi-shade. Its stems are rather lax and need support, which will have to be quite substantial in windy places. In very rich soil it can become invasive but many gardeners will think it impossible to have too much of a good thing. It may be propagated by division. *A. aurea* (syn. *A. aurantiaca*) is a species from Chile, similar in all respects to the above except that it has flowers of a fine warm orange with a yellow throat splashed with maroon stripes.

Alstroemeria psittacina

Alstroemeria psittacina
Origin: Brazil
Height: 24in/60cm
Z: 8

❧ This is a beautiful and strange late-flowering plant of striking colour. The leaves are mid-green, rounded, 3in/8cm long, and the flowers, in July or August, are carried in bold groups at the tips of wiry stems that have a purple bloom. The flowers are the shape of slender trumpets, 2in/5cm long, a lively raspberry colour with mysterious green tips to the petals which have deep purple stripes within. It is a very decorative plant in a place of prominence in a narrow border where it must have a sunny site and well-drained soil. It is easily propagated by division.

Anemone

There are about seventy species of anemone, in the family Ranunculaceae, all herbaceous perennials. Those with tuberous roots are described below; those with fibrous roots appear on pages 67–8 under 'Herbaceous Perennials'.

Anemone blanda
Origin: E. Mediterranean
H: 6in/15cm
Z: 5

❧ Both its foliage and flowers make this an essential spring plant. The leaves are many-lobed and deeply cut, forming an exceptionally attractive background to the flowers which appear in March. These are 2in/5cm across, single but with many petals that spread out in the sun. The colour of the flowers is extremely variable from pale to deep blue (always with a hint of violet) and white. The white form is especially decorative; the backs of the petals, perfectly visible when the flower is closed, are flushed with a pale creamy pink. It is easy to cultivate, with no particular soil requirements but at its best in dappled shade, and it is extremely hardy, flourishing in the wild up to 6,000ft/1,800m. There is a good pure white cultivar, 'White Splendour', and a fine rich blue, 'Atrocaerulea'. All are perfect for the small garden and form an admirable background to other spring plantings.

Arum

Arum italicum italicum
(A.i. marmoratum)
Origin: S. Europe
Height: 18in/45cm
Z: 6

There are twelve species of arum, in the family Araceae, native to Europe and the Mediterranean.

❧ The foliage of this arum, by far its chief distinction, appears in autumn and lasts through the winter into early summer. Each leaf is shaped like an irregular spearhead, up to 12in/30cm long and 6in/15cm broad at its widest point. Deep green, undulating and beautifully marbled with grey veins, they provide a brilliant background to more colourful plants such as hellebores, which also enjoy a shady place and moist soil. The unexciting flowers appear in spring and in autumn; occasionally spires of berries, a brilliant scarlet, appear simultaneously with the new leaves. It may be propagated by division in late summer.

Asphodeline

Asphodeline lutea
Origin: Mediterranean
Height: 36in/90cm
Z: 7

There are about twenty species of asphodeline, in the family Liliaceae/Asphodelaceae, native to the Mediterranean countries.

❧ The yellow asphodel is an exotic and striking plant. The leaves are very narrow, like grass, a distinguished silver-glaucous colour, and, from the moment they appear as swirling silver rosettes in early spring, very decorative. From their midst the flowering stems erupt in May, culminating in long flowering heads covered in star-like rich yellow flowers, each up to 2in/5cm across. It has great architectural presence in a border at a time when herbaceous plants have yet to make an impact; furthermore its fine foliage continues to be ornamental throughout the season. There is an especially good double-flowered form, 'Florepleno'. Asphodels need a sunny position and prefer light well-drained soil. They may be propagated by seed (the pods are very decorative) or by division.

Camassia

Camassia leichtlinii
Origin: W. North America
Height: 24–36in/
60–90cm
Z: 3

A genus of about five species of the family Liliaceae/Hyacinthaceae, all of which are natives of North America. Their common name, quamash, is an Indian name. They are exceptionally good plants for the border where, in suitable conditions, they may flourish undisturbed for many years. Long-established clumps may be divided to produce further bulbs. The foliage dies in the late summer so place them where other plants may conceal the dying leaves.

❧ In April flowering shoots emerge from among the glistening dark green foliage. They are very dark, almost black, and the flower heads resemble a giant head of wheat without the whiskers. Flowers open in May, starting at the base of the head and working upwards, dazzling purple-blue, white or creamy yellow stars with slender petals; there is also a double-flowered form. The petals intertwine curiously as they wither. This wonderful border plant will relish rich moist soil and semi-shade.

Camassia quamash
Origin: W. North America
Height: 24–36in/
60–90cm
Z: 5

🌱 Tufts of decorative strap-like leaves appear in the spring and, in May or June, tall stems bear striking dark blue star-shaped flowers of sprightly character. In the wild this camassia is found in a wide range of different habitats, from the very dry to the very wet, and it will do well in light shade. The flowers look beautiful against silver or grey foliage such as that of artemisias or santolinas.

Chionodoxa

Chionodoxa luciliae
Origin: W. Turkey
Height: 2¹/₂in/7.5cm
Z: 4

A genus of around five species in the family Liliaceae/Hyacinthaceae, all of which are native to the eastern Mediterranean and in particular to Turkey. The species described below is truly garden worthy.

🌱 Chionodoxa means 'glory of the snow', and in its native habitat it is found in mountainous regions near the snow line where it starts to flower with the first thaw. In more temperate lowland places it will flower in February or March, the small star-shaped flowers held aloft, a piercing lavender-blue with a pale eye, above fresh green leaves. It is not choosy as to soil and although flowering at its best in a sunny position will perform adequately in light shade. In the garden it will naturalize easily and provide a dazzling blue carpet spreading about, for example, white *Anemone blanda* or the more delicate varieties of pale yellow narcissi.

Convallaria

This is a genus of a single species in the family Liliaceae/Convallariaceae, very widely distributed in the temperate parts of the northern hemisphere.

Convallaria majalis
Origin: North America, Asia, Europe
Height: 10in/25cm
Z: 3

ã In conditions that please it the lily-of-the-valley can become invasive but there are few more beautiful invaders than this. Shoots appear in April, nosing above the ground, grey-green and rather edible in appearance. The leaves unfold – glaucous, elegantly creased, rounded and pointed, 6in/15cm long. They point in different directions, creating the illusion of movement, like a frozen choppy sea. Above them sprays of flowers appear in May: dangling greenish-white balls opening into diminutive bells insignificant in appearance but exuding one of the most delicious of all garden scents – sweet, pure, intense and fresh. It likes a shady position in damp soil and looks wonderful with ferns, marbled *Arum italicum italicum*, and the bold leaves of *Helleborus orientalis*. There are pink, double-flowered and variegated forms, none of which improves on the perfection of the type. It is easily propagated by dividing the rhizomes in autumn.

Crinum

Crinum × powellii
Origin: Garden
Height: 30in/75cm
Z: 6

Illustration opposite:
Crinum × powellii 'Album'

A genus of 130 species, all bulbous, in the family Liliaceae/Amaryllidaceae, very widely distributed in the warmer countries.

❧ This is one of the most spectacular of flowering bulbs. The strap-like leaves are glistening green, up to 36in/90cm long, but sprawling elegantly rather than standing stiffly erect. The flowers in August are carried on fleshy stems, several bold sweetly scented trumpets, up to 4in/10cm long, pale pink and elegantly carried on a curving stem. It must have a very sunny dry position; the foot of a south-facing wall is ideal. It may be propagated by division. There is a beautiful white-flowered form, *C. × p.* 'Album'.

Crocosmia

There are about seven species of crocosmia, formerly known as montbretia, in the family Iridaceae, native to South Africa. All may be propagated by division of the corms.

Crocosmia 'Citronella'
Origin: Garden
Height: 18in/45cm
Z: 6

❧ There is some doubt as to the identity of this lovely plant. The one I grow, long established in the garden, is a plant of exquisite poise. The foliage is upright, narrow and pale green, and the curving flower stems rise a little taller, bearing in August or September sprays of delicate pale yellow flowers of cool and irresistible beauty. It looks marvellous with the grey foliage and blue flowers of *Caryopteris × clandonensis*. It needs sun and is best in light soil.

Crocosmia ×
crocosmiiflora
Origin: Garden
Height: 24in/60cm
Z: 5

❧ The most commonly seen crocosmia, a
19th-century hybrid, is still an admirable border plant.
The slightly curving mid-green pointed foliage makes
splendid lively sheaf-like forms above which the
flowering stems carry their intricate orange-yellow
flowers in July. It will grow well in shade and naturally
forms a gently spreading colony.

Crocosmia ×
crocosmiiflora

Crocosmia 'Lucifer'
Origin: Garden
Height: 4ft/1.2m
Z: 5

❧ The foliage of this magnificent crocosmia is
splendid: bold, upright blade-like leaves coming to a
sharp point and fully 4ft/1.2m tall. The flowers in July,
shapely open trumpets of beautiful deep red with hints
of orange and with an elegantly contrasting yellow
base, are carried in fortissimo sprays, up to 6in/15cm
long, each with many flowers along its length. The
foliage has great presence and the glowing colour of the
flowers is wonderful among hot colours.

Crocos

Illustration opposite:
Crocus tommasinianus

A genus of around eighty species in the family
Iridaceae, native to the Mediterranean countries,
eastern Europe and the Near East. Some of the modern
cultivars are coarse and overblown but the species, and
forms and cultivars close to them, are among the most
attractive and irresistible of garden plants, a thrilling
sight in early spring when little else is performing.
Among the species, none is ugly, many are ravishingly
beautiful, but some are not easy to grow. The exquisite

Crocus gargaricus from Turkey, for example, a wonderful warm saffron yellow, really needs a frame to flourish properly. Keen gardeners will not be put off by this and species crocuses are one of the best plants for the owner of a small garden to collect. I have chosen a few which may be relied upon to perform in average garden conditions to give the true crocus experience.

Crocus gargaricus

Crocus chrysanthus
Origin: E. Europe
Height: 3in/8cm
Z: 4

❧ This little yellow crocus, from the hills of eastern Europe, has given rise to several beautiful cultivars which enjoy a well-drained position in full sun. They will flower in February or March. 'Blue Pearl' is a good blue with ghostly silver within; 'E.A. Bowles' has warm golden yellow flowers with bronze colouring on the back; 'Snow Bunting' is a soft creamy white with smudges of lavender on the back.

Crocus tommasinianus
Origin: E. Europe
Height: 4in/10cm
Z: 5

❧ The appearance of this crocus in early February never fails to lift the winter gloom. The flowers vary in colour from a pale smoky lavender to deep purple, with a pale grey exterior; their rich saffron-orange stamens, incidentally, have a pronounced scent of saffron. The foliage, long slender needles with a pale green stripe, contribute much to the elegance of the flower. In the wild *C. tommasinianus* is found in woodland and shady places and, given such a site in the garden, will naturalize prolifically, providing one of the most disarmingly attractive sights of the early spring, flowering at the same time as snowdrops, winter aconites and the first *Anemone blanda*. There is a white form, *C.t. albus*, which is particularly beautiful.

Crocus vernus albiflorus
Origin: S. Europe
Height: 4in/10cm
Z: 4

❧ Many cultivars have been produced from this crocus which naturally ranges in colour from white to purple. It resembles *C. tommasinianus* but does not have the distinctive pale exterior; instead it has a dark base to the flower head and many of the cultivars are very attractively striped (for example 'Pickwick'). It is are excellent for naturalizing.

Cyclamen

A genus of nine species in the family Primulaceae, native to Mediterranean countries. Of the hardy kinds described below all, if given the conditions they like, will settle down and form colonies to provide some of the most beautiful and trouble-free plantings in the garden. Almost any garden will find a habitat to suit them. The three species described here cover a flowering period from late summer to spring, and even when not in flower their finely patterned foliage is exceptionally decorative.

Cyclamen coum

Cyclamen coum
Origin: E. Europe, the
Caucasus and the Near
East
Height: $2^1/_2$in/6cm
Z: 6

❧ *Cyclamen coum* has decorative small rounded leaves, $1^1/_2$in/4cm across, with wonderful, variable mottled patterns. The delicate flowers, no more than $^1/_2$in/1.25cm in length, tipped with deep carmine at the bottom, vary in colour from lively purple-pinks to rich magenta and appear in February. This is the spring counterpart of *Cyclamen hederifolium* and consorts beautifully with the season's aconites, *Anemone blanda*, crocuses and snowdrops – a dazzling tapestry. Rich soil in a partly shaded place will suit it best and allow it to naturalize freely. A white form, *C.c. album*, is especially beautiful, looking wonderful with pale violet *Crocus tommasinianus*.

Cyclamen hederifolium
(*C. neapolitanum*)
Origin: S. Europe and
E. Mediterranean
Height: $2^1/_2$in/6cm
Z: 6

❧ In late summer and autumn the sharp carmine flowers of this cyclamen, borne on slender stems above leafless corms, are one of the delights of the season. The flowers are followed by leaves of exceptional beauty, mottled and marbled in tones of silvery green and grey,

shaped like ivy but of infinitely greater elegance. These, variable in shape, pattern and colour, will in time form spreading mats of foliage, making a brilliant winter ornament and providing in the spring the perfect backgound to the smaller bulbs that flower in that season. They also look well planted at the foot of deciduous trees or large shrubs. Given the rich moist soil they like, and a partly shaded position, they will naturalize readily. They may not spread so obligingly in drier places but will flower perfectly well; in my own garden they sparkle in the shade of a fresh green box hedge. The white form, *C.h. album*, is equally beautiful. Small seedlings may be transplanted very easily when in leaf.

Cyclamen repandum

Cyclamen repandum
Origin: N.E. Mediterranean
Height: 2in/5cm
Z: 7

&❧ The boldly decorative leaves of this cyclamen are loosely heart-shaped with scalloped edges, up to 5in/12cm across, marked with paler colouring towards the centre. The flowers in May are a dazzling magenta, held well above the leaves, and wonderfully scented with a warm sweet perfume that on a sunny spring day can carry far across the garden. In the wild it is found in shady places and in the garden it looks beautiful in mossy woodland places where it will naturalize easily. It is not as often seen as the two species described above, which it easily rivals in beauty *and* it has a delicious scent.

Eranthis

There are about seven species of eranthis, in the family Ranunculaceae, of which the one described is, once established, an essential trouble-free plant of late winter.

Eranthis hyemalis
Origin: W. Europe
Height: 2–3in/5–8cm
Z: 5

The winter aconite has rich gleaming buttercup-yellow flowers 1in/2.5cm across, suspended aloft above a ruff of elegant foliage. The flower buds emerge from the soil, thrusting heads of yellow, bringing light to dull winter days. In the wild it is found in woodland and scrub, in deep rich soil. In the garden it will do best in a shady, or partly shaded position, and it makes a marvellous golden carpet about the trunks of deciduous trees. It will naturalize easily by self-seeding and it may be increased by dividing clumps after flowering.

Eremurus

There are about fifty species of eremurus, all herbaceous rhizomes, in the family Liliaceae/Asphodelaceae, native to Asia.

Eremurus robustus
Origin: Afghanistan, Russia
Height: 8ft/2.5m
Z: 5

The immense flowering spires of this eremurus, at once spectacular but delicate, are a marvellous sight. The leaves are a fresh green, 1 1/2in/4cm wide, strap-like. The flower stems soar aloft, bearing long flower heads smothered in June with diminutive very

pale pink flowers. Sometimes the flower heads will twist into dramatic curved shapes. This is a wonderful plant for the back of a grand border where it will hold its own in even the most distinguished company. It must have rich moist soil in a sunny place and it will certainly need support. It may be propagated by division.

Erythronium

There are about twenty species of erythronium, in the family Liliaceae/Liliaceae, widely dispersed in Europe, Japan and North America. They are exceptionally distinguished plants, introducing an exotic but elegant note to the spring garden. Not the easiest of plants to cultivate, they nevertheless more than repay the effort. All may be propagated by dividing clumps after flowering when the foliage is still green.

Eythronium dens-canis
Origin: Asia, S. Europe
Height: 6in/15cm
Z: 3

❧ The dog's tooth violet has a striking combination of mottled foliage and glamorous little flowers. The leaves, 3in/8cm long and with striking patterns of purplish mottling, appear in March or April, followed by the flowers, pinkish-purple, 1 $^{1}/_{2}$in/4cm long, with petals curving sharply backwards. In the wild this is a plant of deciduous woodland and in the garden it will be successful at the feet of deciduous early spring-flowering shrubs like corylopsis or witch hazel. There are several cultivars but none to beat the charm and purity of the type.

Erythronium tuolumnense

Erythronium tuolumnense
Origin: California
H: 10in/25cm
Z: 5

❧ The foliage of this erythronium, a glistening mid-green, has undulating edges, giving a lively wave-like appearance. The single clear yellow flowers appear in March, borne high above, with pointed petals curving backwards, like diminutive lilies. In the wild it grows in woodland, and a partly shaded position will suit it best in the garden.

Erythronium 'White Beauty'
Origin: Garden
H: 6in/15cm
Z: 5

Illustration opposite:
Erythronium 'White Beauty'

❧ This cultivar, of uncertain parentage, is a plant of supreme distinction. Creamy white flowers appear in April above mid-green foliage with decorative 'marbling, as though seen through ripples of water. It flourishes in shade, consorting well with *Helleborus orientalis*, cyclamen and trilliums to form a spring picture of subtlety and liveliness.

Fritillaria

There are about 100 species of fritillaries, in the family Liliaceae/Liliaceae, very widely distributed in the temperate parts of the northern hemisphere. Some are ancient garden plants, of proven value, others have become objects of desire among collectors. Among them are some of the best of all flowering bulbs.

Fritillaria imperialis
Origin: W. Himalaya, Afghanistan, Iran
Height: 3ft/1m
Z: 4

❧ The crown imperial is one of the most imposing of bulbous plants. Its foliage emerges in early March, unfurling thrillingly above the soil, tufts of distinguished glistening pale green. The flower heads in April or May consist of several hanging bell-shaped flowers, warm yellow or orange-brown, up to twenty on a single head, crowned by foliage like the plume on a knight's helmet. The large bulbs, with their pungent, foxy scent which is imparted by the whole plant, should be planted deep (a good 6in/15cm below the surface) and on their sides. In moist soil place them on a good bed of coarse grit to prevent the bulbs from rotting. The crown imperial will flower equally well in partial shade or full sun. Once settled, it will multiply if undisturbed and provide one of the most exquisite of all ornamental plants. There are various fancy cultivars but none improves on the species.

Fritillaria meleagris
Origin: W. Europe
Height: 4–6in/10–15cm
Z: 4

❧ The bell-shaped flowers of the snake's head fritillary, a European native but increasingly rare in the wild, appear in April or May; white or purple-pink with checkerboard pattern, they droop elegantly on slender swaying stems. The plant's natural habitat is damp grassland or light woodland, and in the garden it will do best in a similar situation, naturalizing well, the ornamental seed heads scattering quantities of seed. It looks its best in an informal setting, and if you are lucky enough to have an orchard, they look marvellous massed in rough grass with *Anemone blanda* and pale daffodils in the dappled shade of apple trees.

Fritillaria persica
'Adiyaman'
Origin: Turkey
Height: 24in/60cm
Z: 5

❧ In foliage and flower this is a dazzling plant. The leaves appear in March, a decorative glaucous-grey, slender and slightly twisted, 2–3in/5–8cm long, at right-angles to a fleshy stem. The flowers appear in April or May, a spectacular spire of hanging deep purple bells of wonderful distinction. This is less hardy than *F. imperialis* and needs a sunny well-drained site where it will look marvellous with small shrubs of Mediterranean character like artemisias and cistuses.

Galanthus

A genus of around twelve species in the family Liliaceae/Amaryllidaceae, found in eastern Europe as far east as the Caucasus. From the gardener's point of view there is one essential species, not showy but irresistible, which is described below.

Galanthus nivalis
Origin: E. Europe
Height: 4–5in/10–12.5cm
Z: 4

❧ The common snowdrop, flowering from January onwards, with its hanging white flowers tipped with green, is one of the most cheerful winter sights. In the wild this is a plant of damp woodland or the shady margins of hedgerows, and in the garden it is perhaps at its best tucked into odd corners rather than given a place of prominence in a border. The snowdrop makes a marvellous picture with other winter-flowering plants such as the winter aconite (*Eranthis hyemalis*). Not in the slightest choosy about soil, but flourishing in moisture-retentive earth, clumps of snowdrops may easily be propagated by division immediately after flowering. *G. × atkinsii* is a very handsome large-flowered hybrid with wide-spreading petals. A double-flowered form, *G.n.* 'Flore Pleno', is also found, which I consider much coarser in character than

the unassuming and charming simplicity of the single-flowered kinds. There are other species and many cultivars of great interest to collectors, but none offers any striking advantage over the common snowdrop.

Galtonia

There are three species of galtonia, all bulbs, in the family Liliaceae/Hyacinthaceae, native to South Africa.

Galtonia candicans
Origin: S. Africa
Height: 4ft/1.2m
Z: 7

❧ The great virtue of galtonia is that it flowers very late in the season when the mixed border is starting to flag. The leaves are shaped like blades and the flowers, appearing in July or August, are beautiful. They are bell-shaped, ivory-white, of waxy texture, 2in/5cm long and elegantly hanging, borne in generous spires at the tips of pale pistachio-coloured stems. It needs plenty of sun and light but rich soil. It is very versatile in a mixed border where it should be planted in bold groups – I have seen it used spectacularly mixed with pale creamy orange lilies and with pale blue agapanthus. It may be propagated by division or seeds.

Gladiolus

There are about 180 species of gladiolus, in the family Iridaceae, widely distributed in the warmer regions of Africa, Asia and Europe. That described below is one of the very few properly hardy in cooler areas.

Gladiolus communis
Origin: Mediterranean
Height: 36in/90cm
Z: 6

ᙍStiff blade-like curving leaves are the first sign of this showy gladiolus coming to life in April. In late May or June the curving flower buds, like the beaks of an exotic bird, explode – and that is the right word – into brilliant colour. The flowers are loud magenta trumpets, 2in/5cm long, striped with white in their throats. This is a plant for the bold border that makes a virtue of reds and purples. It likes a sunny, dry site where it will seed itself satisfyingly. For more timid gardeners there is a fine white form, *G. c.* 'Albus'.

Hemerocallis

There are about fifteen species of daylily, in the family Liliaceae/Hemerocallidaceae, all native to east Asia. This is one of most hybridized of all groups of garden plants, with many thousands of listed cultivars and hundreds of new ones introduced every year, especially in the USA where they are immensely popular. Virtually every colour is now available and, as far as the gardener is concerned, it is merely a matter of choosing the right colour for a particular scheme. Having said that, some of the old varieties, and some of the species, although available only in a restricted colour range, are still wonderful garden plants, with beauty of form and scent allied to quality of colour. They are among the easiest to please of all really beautiful perennial plants. They need a certain amount of sun but will thrive in semi-shade, and a moist soil suits them best. Each flower, of course, lasts a brief time, but they are produced in generous succession over a long period. All have glistening strap-like leaves which in themselves are very handsome, making an admirable background to other plantings. Clumps tend to become congested, which inhibits flowering, and they will flower at their best if they are divided every three or four years – which is the simplest way of propagation.

Hemerocallis fulva

Hemerocallis citrina
Origin: China
Height: 36in/90cm
Z: 4

❦ This species has an especially fine clear pale lemon colour and a wonderful sweet scent. The flowers are 4in/10cm long and open from June onwards. The petals are well separated, and pointed, with green stripes down the back and slightly undulating margins, giving a liveliness to what might have been a rather stiff flower. Its whole character is one of lightness. I have seen it looking very beautiful surrounded by waves of creamy yellow *Anthemis tinctoria* 'E.C. Buxton'.

Hemerocallis fulva
Origin: Japan
Height: 36in/90cm
Z: 4

❦ This Japanese daylily has long been cultivated in gardens in the west. It has a particularly vigorous, healthy appearance, and flowers in July are borne in successive profusion over a long period. They are large, up to 5in/13cm across, of a fine rusty orange, fading to yellow deep in the throat, with the elegantly pointed petals curving strongly back. There is an especially striking double-flowered cultivar, *H.f.* 'Flore Pleno'; a double flower is not always an improvement but in this case it gives an exuberant and exotic character to the plant. In a border of hot colours it looks splendidly dramatic but it is not for the faint-hearted.

Hermodactylus

This is a genus of a single species in the family Iridaceae.

Hermodactylus tuberosus
Origin: S. Europe
H: 9in/22.5cm
Z: 7

❧ The snake's head, or widow iris is a plant of sinister distinction. The bud emerges from stems like tall grass, pointed and triangular like a long spearhead. The three petals, appearing in March or April, curve back, tipped in velvety black, to reveal a throat of glistening green-gold. It has a fugitive but distinctive sweet scent. It is easy to cultivate and may be propagated by dividing the tubers in the summer after flowering. Few bulbous plants flowering at this time of year have quite the aristocratic air possessed by this. In the garden it will easily upstage less distinguished plants and is at its best in a border backed by some evergreen small shrub such as cistus or sarcococca against whose foliage the exotic flowers may be properly appreciated.

Iris

There are over 200 species of irises, belonging to the family Iridaceae, very widely distributed in the northern hemisphere. Many of them are among the most beautiful of all flowering plants. They are either bulbs or rhizomes; the latter provide the easier garden plants and have been the subject of tremendous interest from nurserymen who have bred countless cultivars of, in particular, the bearded irises. These derive their name from the patch of hairy down on the inside of the petals and range in size from Miniature Dwarf Bearded (5–7in/13–18cm high) to Tall Bearded (up to 30in/90cm). These attractive plants exist in an immense range of colours, with especially beautiful creamy yellows and soft blues. They are hardy (Zone 5), flower from May onwards in a sunny position, and are very easy to propagate by dividing the rhizomes in late summer. This should be done every three or four years as old clumps flower poorly. There is little point in naming particular cultivars; it is a matter of choosing the right colour for your scheme from the huge range available in garden centres.

Some of the bulbous irises, for example the lovely scented yellow *Iris danfordiae* and the intense blue *Iris reticulata*, both flowering very early in the year, are very demanding as to cultivation and are probably best in the carefully tended rock or trough garden. It is certainly very difficult to establish them permanently in the border. But the species that follow, all rhizomes, may be depended upon to perform without fuss.

Iris douglasiana

Iris douglasiana
Origin: W. North America
Height: 24in/60cm
Z: 7

❧ This is one of the beautiful tribe of Pacific Coast irises and is an exceptionally decorative, and easy, garden plant. From a mound of grass-like glistening foliage the flowering stems rise high aloft in May. The flowers are 4in/10cm across, with graceful backward-curving petals and decorative slightly ruffled margins. They vary in colour but the commonest is a rich violet-blue, with an intricate network of deeper coloured veins fading to ivory white on the inside of the petals, and smudges of yellow in the throat. There are various named cultivars, some of them in rather strident colours, and an especially good white one, *I.d.* 'Alba'. It flourishes in well-drained soil in a partly shaded site.

Iris sibirica
Origin: N. Asia, E. Europe
Height: 36in/90cm
Z: 4

❧ Striking slender blade-like leaves announce the Siberian iris in spring. The flowers, rising well above the foliage, open in May, neat and elegant, a rich purple-blue, up to 5in/12.5cm long. There are several excellent white cultivars and many hybrids with *I. sanguinea*, producing a wide range of colours and, in some cases, rather overblown flowers. This is a marvellous plant for moist soil at the water's edge but it will flower perfectly well in the border where it prefers a heavy soil in a sunny position.

Iris sibirica

Iris unguicularis
(*I. stylosa*)
Origin: N. Africa,
E. Mediterranean
Height: 10in/25cm
Z: 7

❧The Algerian iris will flourish in poor soil in any dry, sunny corner of the garden. Most gardens will be able to find a place to suit it and every gardener should do so; it is a plant of irresistible beauty. Plant it at the foot of a wall or, as I have it, at the foot of a bush of rosemary, where it contrasts well with the grey-green foliage. According to the weather, it may produce flowers at any time from December to March. These, a clear pale lavender with smudges of primrose-yellow and white stripes at the throat, 4in/10cm across and borne on slender stems, lie half hidden among the pointed strap-like foliage that rises above them. They are easily propagated by dividing clumps at any time after flowering but they may take two or three years to settle down and flower reliably. There is a rare white form, *I.u. alba*, that is worth seeking out, and several named cultivars of varying shades of violet which scarcely improve on the type. Dead foliage should be removed and some gardeners believe that cutting back the foliage in late spring encourages flowering.

Kniphofia

Kniphofia 'Goldelse'

There are about sixty species of kniphofia, or red hot poker, all herbaceous rhizomes in the family Liliaceae/Asphodelaceae, all native to Africa. The commonly seen cultivar, with tall flower stems crowned with heads like lollipops, half orange and half yellow, is a cheerful but rather coarse plant and very difficult to fit into other schemes. But there are several excellent yellow-flowered varieties that make beautiful late summer plants. 'Goldelse' has lime-green flower heads on stems up to 4ft/1.2m which as they grow to full size (up to 6in/15cm long) turn to soft golden-yellow. The foliage is splendidly decorative, profuse triangular reed-like leaves that curve gracefully. All are hardy to Zone 8 and though they must have a warm position in light free-draining soil will flower in part shade. They may be propagated by division. 'Green Jade' is similar but preserves a distinguished green cast in the mature flower, and 'Snow Maiden' is a very handsome creamy white.

Leucojum

There are about ten species of the snowflake, in the family Liliaceae/Amaryllidaceae, close cousins of the snowdrop. They are much larger, and more striking, and in the garden have a more emphatic presence. They may be propagated by division.

Leucojum aestivum
Origin: Europe
Height: 24in/60cm
Z: 4

❧ The summer snowflake, which flowers from late spring to early summer, is like a giant snowdrop appearing at the wrong time of year. Its hanging white snowdrop-like flowers, tipped with green, rise above a profusion of foliage. An especially good form, *L.a.* 'Gravetye Giant', has several flowers on each stem, a more upright habit than the type, and makes an excellent border plant for the early summer.

Leucojum vernum

Leucojum vernum
Origin: Europe
Height: 5–6in/12.5–15cm
Z: 4

❧ The spring snowflake has distinctive hanging white flowers, in shape resembling a blowsy lampshade, their petals tipped with greenish-yellow. They appear in early spring above shining strap-like foliage, nodding in the breeze. In the wild the snowflake is a plant of woodland or shady hedgerows and it likes rich moist soil. It will naturalize easily but clumps may be divided after flowering when the foliage is still green. Although a splendid plant for a wild woodland garden it has enough cool elegance for the front of a shady border where it looks wonderful rising above blue *Anemone blanda* or among the reddish emerging stems of herbaceous peonies.

Lilium

There are about 100 species of lily, in the family Liliaceae/Liliaceae, widely distributed in the temperate parts of the northern hemisphere. Lilies have the not unjustified reputation of being difficult to cultivate in the garden. Many gardeners have had the experience of planting dozens of expensive bulbs to be rewarded with only one successful flowering season. But few difficult plants are more worth persevering with. Most lilies need a combination of good drainage, plenty of moisture during the growing season and plenty of nourishment. They make marvellous ornaments both in the border and in the wilder setting of a woodland garden. They are excellent for pots, where it is easier to provide exactly the conditions that suit them. There are immense numbers of cultivars, some with impossibly strident colours and excessively elaborate flowers. I have concentrated here on a few species that would ornament any garden.

Lilium candidum
Origin: Greece
Height: 5ft/1.5m
Z: 6

❧ The Madonna lily is one of the most anciently cultivated garden plants. The tall stems are covered in upward-pointing leaves, and the flowers are grouped at the top of the stem in great abundance. They open in June, crisp white trumpet shapes up to 4in/10cm long, with backward-curving petals, giving off an intense sweet perfume. The plants are, however, prone to virus infection, and the best clumps are often seen in gardens where no other lily is grown. Unlike other lilies the bulbs should be planted very near the surface, where they benefit from baking in the sun. They may be propagated by seed which germinates easily.

Lilium pardalinum
Origin: W. North America
Height: 6ft/1.8m
Z: 5

❧ I love the exotic and elegant panther lily. It throws up very tall stems with the leaves arranged in ruffs along its length. Downward-hanging orange-flushed buds open in June or July into spectacular 3in/8cm long lantern-like flowers. The petals curve back upon themselves, red-brown at the tips but in the throat yellow spotted with maroon markings. Very long stamens protrude, carrying chocolate-brown stigmas. I grow this in completely the wrong place in dry rather poor soil at the foot of a sunny wall but it needs a moister, richer soil to give of its best.

Lilium regale

Lilium regale
Origin: China
Height: 5ft/1.5m
Z: 5

❧ This is one of the commonest lilies and still one of the best. The tall stems have short spiky leaves and culminate in June or July in magnificent flowers. The long pink-purple buds open into splendid trumpets, up to 5in/13cm long, opening widely at the end, white but striped on the back with purple-pink and with a pale golden throat and striking orange stamens. The scent is one of the very best – heavy, sweet and intense; it is especially powerful in the late afternoon and early

Illustration opposite:
Lilium pardalinum

evening as the air begins to cool. Plant it in generous clumps near a sitting place. It looks magnificent with the larger wild roses and I have seen it grown spectacularly with the great arching shoots of *Rosa moyesii*. It may be propagated from seed from which flowering bulbs may be raised in about two years.

Lilium speciosum album

Lilium speciosum album
Origin: Japan
Height: 3–5ft/1–1.5m
Zone: 5

❧ This great Japanese lily flowers later than most and is magnificently scented. The flowers open in August, bold white trumpets whose petals, each up to 4in/10cm long, curve back strikingly in a swaggering arch. Some clones are flushed with varying degrees of crimson; all have very prominent anthers, a deep egg-yolk yellow. It is variable in height but the flowers are always carried profusely on the slender stems, giving a feeling of floriferous abundance. It is an excellent border plant, making an ornamental impact when the main flowering season is drawing to an end.

Narcissus

There are about fifty species of the genus, which belongs to the family Liliaceae/Amaryllidaceae, native to the Mediterranean countries and south Europe. Most commonly grown are the countless cultivars (of which well over 10,000 named varieties exist), which have been bred from the wild European

N. pseudonarcissus. Of these I regard most as large clumsy plants, their flowers a bright but bilious yellow. They are much used in public planting schemes and certainly give large areas of cheerful colour. In the average garden, where attention is more easily focussed on the detail of a plant, both the size and colour of these big brassy daffodils are overpowering and impossible to harmonize with other plantings. Furthermore, they have substantial foliage which lingers long after flowering, providing an unlovely browning clump of tatty leaves which must be left until they are quite dead, for while green they provide essential nourishment for the bulbs. Many of the species narcissi, however, and those hybrids and cultivars close to them, suffer from none of the defects I have mentioned, and have virtues (such as delicious scent) rarely possessed by their more distant cousins.

I shall pick out a few cultivars that seem to me to be especially worthwhile: 'February Gold' (10in/25cm high) is an early flowerer (though very rarely in February!) with elegantly crimped edges to its warm

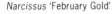

Narcissus 'February Gold'

primrose-yellow trumpet, and well-separated paler petals; 'February Silver' is a paler version. 'Pencrebar' (6in/15cm high) is a late-flowering variety with restrained double flowers of a warm true yellow; 'Thalia' (14in/35cm high) is a wonderful soft white, producing several flowers on each stem, with a trumpet that opens out revealing hints of green-gold within, sweetly scented (14in/35cm high).

The species are much less often seen and yet they are ideal bulbs for the small garden. Many have a delicacy of form and colour, and foliage that dies more gracefully than that of the large cultivars. *N. asturiensis* (4in/10cm high), native to Spain and Portugal, is the quintessential miniature daffodil, with delicate warm yellow hanging flowers appearing very early in January in favoured spots. The jonquil (*N. jonquilla*) (12in/30cm high) from Spain has intensely sweet rich yellow flowers in late spring, only 1in/2.5cm across, carried on slender rush-like stems with grass-like foliage (12in/30cm high). The poet's narcissus, or pheasant's eye (*N. poeticus*) (14in/35cm high) has a spicy scent and exceptionally beautiful flowers, a golden corona tipped in red with graceful white petals sweeping behind. It flowers very late in the spring and early summer. *N. tazetta*, native to the Mediterranean region (12in/30cm high), with several delicate flowers

Narcissus asturiensis

Narcissus 'Geranium'

on each stem, is not very hardy (Zone 8) but there are fine cultivars such as 'Geranium' which are cold-resistant. *N. triandrus*, angel's tears, from France, Portugal and Spain (4in/10cm high), has white or creamy yellow flowers, with petals straining backwards. It flowers in February and, unlike most narcissi, prefers a well-drained position.

All the narcissi described here are hardy to Zone 4 except where otherwise indicated. Most are suitable for naturalizing in grass but the smaller species may be swamped. They like rich moist soil and many will increase in number without any assistance. They should always be planted in naturalistic swathes or clumps; groups of six is the absolute minimum. In an orchard, underplanting fruit trees, they are marvellous intermingled with violet and white *Anemone blanda.* The smaller yellow kinds look wonderful with the blues of chionodoxas and scillas.

Nectaroscordum

There are three species of nectaroscordum, in the family Liliaceae/Alliaceae, native to Asia Minor and southern Europe.

Nectaroscordum siculum
(*Allium siculum*)
Origin: Asia Minor,
S.E.Europe
Height: 5ft/1.5m
Z: 6

❧ There is something distinctly onion-like, both in smell and appearance, in this lovely plant. The foliage is insignificant but in June the tall swaying stems burst into life with their curious flowers. They are carried in generous bunches, each flower bud erect and pointed

Illustration opposite:
Nectaroscordum siculum

but opening into countless hanging bell shapes, cream and green but flushed with red. Later in the season the upward-pointing seed pods are ornamental but may be removed before they are fully ripened, to prevent excessive seeding. It may be grown in sun or semi-shade, and is at its best in a crowded border where the flower stems may rise above other plantings.

Nerine

Nerine bowdenii
Origin: South Africa
Height: 24in/60cm
Z: 8

There are thirty species of nerine, in the family Liliaceae/Amaryllidaceae, native to South Africa.

❧ Flowering in the late autumn, these spectacular bulbs bring an exotic beauty to gardens that can provide the conditions they like. The flowers, a beautiful rich silvery pink, are trumpet-shaped 4in/10cm long, with petals that curl elegantly backwards at their tips. On a crisp day in October or November they provide one of the loveliest garden ornaments you could see. The leaves, strap-like and shining green, appear after flowering. It absolutely demands a sunny site in sharply drained soil: the foot of a south- or west-facing wall is ideal. There is much hybridizing and excellent new cultivars are constantly appearing, often with very large flower heads and

dramatic colours; some, alas, are very susceptible to virus infections. There is an exceptionally beautiful white form, *N.b.* 'Alba'. They may be propagated by division but will take a year or two to settle down and flower properly.

Ornithogalum

There are about eighty species of ornithogalum, in the family Liliaceae/Hyacinthaceae, very widely distributed in Africa, Asia and Europe. Both the species described below may be naturalized in grass where they make excellent successors to the earlier spring-flowering bulbs.

Ornithogalum nutans
Origin: S. Europe
Height: 12in/30cm
Z: 6

❧ This ghostly and distinguished plant will naturalize easily in partial shade and soil that is not too moist. From prolific grass-like foliage curious flower buds erupt in April, resembling large ears of wheat. They open out in late April or May into spires of exquisite single white bell-shaped flowers, striped with grey-green on the outside and sweetly scented with the perfume of honey. There is no explanation for the relative rarity of this bulb in gardens, for it is very easy to please and consorts admirably with other plantings.

Ornithogalum umbellatum
Origin: Mediterranean
Height: 9in/22.5cm
Z: 5

❧ The star of Bethlehem has distinguished glaucous leaves which emerge in April, 4in/10cm long, slender ovals coming to a sharp point. The cheerful star-shaped flowers in May are white, single, with a decorative yellow-tipped corolla and green stripes on the backs of the petals, several on each stem. It will flower well in shade, where its glowing white is seen to great effect.

Polygonatum

There are thiry species of polygonatum, in the family Liliaceae/Convallariaceae, distributed in the temperate regions of the northern hemisphere.

Polygonatum × hybridum
Origin: Garden
Height: 24in/60cm
Z: 6

❧ Solomon's seal appears in March, dove-grey shoots piercing the soil and unfolding creased and slightly twisting leaves. These, 3in/8cm long, spread horizontally from the stems, making a striking pattern when caught by the light. Its hanging white pouch-like flowers, 1in/2.5cm long, appear in April, not exciting but quietly elegant. It relishes rich soil in semi-shade and makes an excellent partner for other foliage plants such as hostas which enjoy the same conditions. There is a rather mean variegated form, *P. × h.* 'Variegatum', which lacks the vigour of the type. It may be propagated by division.

Puschkinia

Puschkinia scilloïdes
Origin: Caucasus
Height: 6in/15cm
Z: 5

There is one species of the genus puschkinia, in the family Liliaceae.

❧ This is a brilliant spring bulb whose pale blue flowers emerge in February or March, borne in profuse bunches above glistening strap-like leaves. Better even than the type is the white form, *P. s. alba,* whose dazzling froth of white seems the very essence of spring. It is best in a sunny well-drained position where it will naturally increase, by seed or bulbils.

Sanguinaria canadensis
'Plena'

Sanguinaria

Sanguinaria canadensis
Origin: North America
Height: 5in/12.5cm
Z: 3

There is only one species of sanguinaria, in the family Papaveraceae.

❧ Blood-root has a cool beauty unlike that of any other plant. It emerges from the soil in April, a pale grey fleshy stem from which flowers and foliage elegantly unfold. The flowers are single, the whitest of white, opening before the leaves have fully unfurled, 1½in/4cm across. The leaves are so decorative that they alone would earn its place in the garden: rounded and lobed, 3in/8cm across, and cupped upwards, a mottled glaucous-grey. It likes light soil, in semi-shade or sun, and is excellent for planting at the feet of deciduous trees or shrubs. A double-flowered form, *S.c.* 'Plena', is very double and exquisitely beautiful.

Scilla

There are about 100 species of scilla, in the family Liliaceae/Hyacinthaceae. They are trouble-free plants, many of which will naturalize freely. One of them, the true European bluebell, *S. non-scripta*, of dazzling beauty in its natural woodland habitat, always seems to me an unhappy garden plant.

Scilla mischtschenkoana
(*S. tubergeniana*)
Origin: Iran
Height: 4–5in/10–12.5cm
Z: 6

ﮯ The flowers of this Persian squill erupt from the naked earth in February or March, opening close to the soil and later thrusting up above shining mid-green leaves like curved blades. Several flowers, 1in/2.5cm across, of the palest blue or bluish-white, with dashing deeper blue veins on the back, hang from the stem, giving the effect of a froth of flowers. Despite its small size there is an cheerful exuberance about *S. mischtschenkoana*, a quintessential spring flower. It likes rich moist soil in a sunny position. Clumps of bulbs may be divided after flowering and will rapidly increase.

Scilla mischtschenkoana

Scilla siberica
Origin: Russia, Siberia, Turkey
Height: 3–4in/8–10cm
Z: 5

ﮯ The Siberian squill is a jaunty little plant, giving splashes of brilliant blue (a richer colour in the shade) in early spring. The diminutive dangling flowers, nodding in a breeze, are at their best in quantity, making a blue carpet and providing a lively background to other spring plantings. They look particularly beautiful with pale lavender or white *Crocus tommasinianus*, white *Anemone blanda*, or the smaller pale yellow or cream daffodils. There is a pretty white form, *S.s.* 'Alba'. Clumps of bulbs may be divided after flowering, but in favourable conditions of cool moist soil it will self-seed with abandon.

Illustration opposite:
Scilla siberica

Smilacina

There are about twenty-five species of smilacina, in the family Liliaceae/Convallariaceae, whose wild habitats are in Central and North America and in Asia.

Smilacina racemosa
Origin: North America
Height: 24in/60cm
Z: 4

❧ False spikenard, a most beautiful North American plant, is one of the finest herbaceous plants for shade or semi-shade. The leaves resemble Solomon's seal, each is 4in/10cm long, furrowed and with twisted margins, appearing on arching stems. The flowers in May are creamy white clusters at the end of the stems, richly perfumed with the sweet scent of freesias. With other shade-loving plants such as the larger ferns this makes a brilliant sight. It is supposedly a lime hater but I have seen it growing satisfactorily in limy soil. At all events, it will perform best in fertile moist soil where it will form a handsome clump. It may be propagated by division in autumn.

Sternbergia

A genus of six species, in the family Amaryllidaceae, of which the one described below is a bulb of dashing character not often enough seen in gardens.

Sternbergia lutea
Origin: Mediterranean Europe
Height: 6in/15cm
Z: 7

❧ The common sternbergia, sometimes misleadingly called an autumn crocus, is a dazzling apparition in September or October. Its flowers, up to 2in/5cm long, are a rich golden yellow with a glistening surface, framed by the shining foliage which rises taller than the

Sternbergia lutea

flowers. No other autumn plant produces this shade of sparkling yellow which goes so well with the tawny colours of autumn foliage. It likes rich moist soil in a sunny position, and in my garden seems to have found the perfect home between old paving stones. Clumps of bulbs may be divided in early spring.

Tricyrtis

Tricyrtis formosana
Origin: Taiwan
Height: 4ft/1.2m
Z: 7

There are about fifteen species of toad-lily, in the family Liliaceae/Convallariaceae, all rhizomatous plants native to east Asia.

ᔐ The toad-lily is a marvellously ornamental plant for late summer. The foliage is very handsome, each leaf up to 4in/10cm long, rounded but narrow, coming to an elegant point at the tip and marked with pronounced veining, running its whole length. The flowers, 1½in/4cm across, which open in late August but continue for weeks, are carried at the tips of stems and are white but almost obliterated with maroon spots. A circle of lemon-yellow runs around inside the thoat and the buds, before opening, are purple-red and covered in a fine fuzz. It is best in rich moist soil and it grows well in part shade. It is very easy to propagate by division.

Tricyrtis formosana

Trillium

Trillium erectum
Origin: North America
Height: 12in/30cm
Z: 4

There are about thirty species of trillium, all herbaceous rhizomes, in the family Liliaceae/Trilliaceae, and native to North America and east Asia. Their name comes from the fact that all species have three-part petals and flowers.

❧ This woodland plant flowers in May and varies in colour from pale wine to a mahogany red. The flowers, borne on upright stems, are 1¹/₂in/4cm long and give off a curious rather foxy odour. The leaves, rounded and pointed at each end, are up to 3in/8cm long. It is best propagated by division in late autumn. It is a plant of sombre distinction that looks marvellous with lilies-of-the-valley or planted in quantity at the feet of *Smilacina racemosa*.

Trillium grandiflorum

Trillium grandiflorum
Origin: North America
Height: 18in/45cm
Z: 4

❧ The wake robin, another woodland plant, makes a superb ornament for a shady border in some wild and informal corner of the garden. Its leaves and flowers unfold simultaneously in late April or May; the dazzlingly white flowers are broadly rounded and pointed, 2^1/$_2$in/4cm long and lightly furrowed, with vivid yellow stamens. A double-flowered form, *T.g. flore-pleno*, is if anything even more beautiful – one of those plants that bowls you over at first sight and never loses its charms. It is fully double, becoming a more creamy white towards the centre. Beware of using it alongside anything much less distinguished. It is easily propagated by division in autumn.

Tristagma

A genus of about ten species of the family Liliaceae/Alliaceae, all native to South America. The genus has been comprehensively kicked about by the botanists, and gardeners may find it hard to keep track of names. It is still widely known as Ipheion.

Tristagma uniflorum
(*Ipheion uniflorum*)
Origin: South America
Height: 5in/12.5cm
Z: 6

❧ The flowers of *Tristagma uniflorum*, handsomely trumpet-shaped, opening in the sun to a star, vary from chalk white to pale violet. Appearing in early spring, 1¹/₂in/4cm across and borne on slender stems above a mass of slender strap-like leaves, they have the savoury smell of onions when crushed, contrasting with the soft, honey scent of the flowers. The petals are violet-striped, back and front, much more striking in the pale forms. In the garden the foliage makes an attractive ground-cover, and the plants will tolerate light shade but will flower best in a sunny position. They are not choosy as to soil, doing well in poor stony earth. In richer soil they may propagate themselves in embarrassing quantities. There are various named cultivars, including a striking rich purple one, *T.u.* 'Froyle Mill'.

Triteleia

There are about fifteen species of triteleia, all corms in the family Liliaceae/Tricyrtidaceae, all from western North America.

Triteleia laxa
Origin: California, Oregon
Height: 12in/30cm
Z: 7

❧ From grass-like leaves slender stems bear profuse umbels of trumpet-shaped flowers in June or July. These are rich purple-blue or white, with pointed petals and a dark stripe down the back of each petal. It must have a sunny position and light soil where it will reproduce gently to form an unthreatening colony. This is one of those valuable ornamental plants that takes up little ground space and will hover decoratively over lower-growing plants such as pinks.

Tulipa 'White Triumphator'

Tulipa

There are more than 100 species of tulips, in the family Liliaceae/Liliaceae, whose natural habitats are in western and central Asia, Europe and north Africa. New cultivars are constantly been introduced. There are many beautiful species which, rarely exceeding 6in/15cm in height, are just not equipped for the hurly-burly of life in the border. They also frequently have very specific cultivation requirements which the average gardener will not be able to supply. The lovely deep lilac *T. bakeri* from Crete, for example, absolutely demands baking sunshine and sharp drainage; it will then seed itself and naturalize easily. However, as a general rule I have found that tulip cultivars quite close to the wild type are not only the most valuable from an ornamental point of view, but also tend to perform better, for many years, than the more intensely hybridized tulips. All those mentioned below are hardy to Zone 5.

Tulipa fosteriana, a brilliant scarlet tulip from central Asia, exists in several oustanding cultivars that make excellent border plants to grow through low-growing permanent shrubs: *T.f.* 'Purissima', a creamy white; *T.f.* 'Candela', a clear pale yellow; and *T.f.* 'Red Emperor,' an excellent scarlet which is wonderful with the purple foliage of coggygria or berberis. The flowers appear in April or May, 3in/8cm long, on stems up to 24in/60cm high.

Tulipa kaufmanniana from central Asia is 3½in/9.5cm high and has striking glaucous foliage with a twisted margin, and in April lemon-yellow flowers brushed with scarlet on their outer sides. It likes a sunny position in light thin soil and will not tolerate water-logged ground.

Tulipa tarda from central Asia is 3in/8cm high and produces creamy white flowers with a spreading lemon throat in April. It likes a sunny position in poor stony soil that is well drained, where it will seed and multiply.

Tulipa tarda

Lily-flowered tulips are tall (up to 24in/60cm) and have long flower buds with more or less pointed flowers which in full sun open out and twist gracefully. 'West Point' is an especially good lemon-yellow with

Tulipa 'Van der Neer'

exceptionally long pointed petals. 'White Triumphator' is an excellent creamy white.

Rembrandt tulips are those intricately striped and marbled in two colours. They hark back to the early 17th-century Dutch cultivars and many of them are very beautiful. They are 24–30in/60–75cm tall and some last many years in the garden. The patterns are caused by a virus which means, in principle, that they should not be grown near other tulips. They like rich moist soil and last much better in semi-shade. 'Dreaming Maid' is white, delicately flecked and striped with pink. 'Prins Carnaval' is yellow with red marbling. 'Van der Neer' is creamy white with deep red edges and marbling.

Uvularia

There are three species of uvularia, all herbaceous rhizomes, in the family Liliaceae/Convallariaceae and native to North America.

Uvularia grandiflora
Origin: North America
Height: 18–24in/
45–60cm
Z: 5

This easy and beautiful plant, flowering in semi-shade, should be much more widely grown. The leaves have something of the character of Solomon's seal: glaucous-green, they dangle, slightly twisted, from grey stems. The lemon-yellow flowers in April or May are 2in/5cm long, a very elegant trumpet shape, pointing downwards with pointed and twisted petals. This is a wonderful companion to ferns, lily-of-the-valley, erythroniums and other plants that relish partial shade; among such decorative foliage the yellow of the uvularia is brilliantly effective. It is easy to propagate by dividing the roots in autumn.

Veratrum

There are about twenty species of veratrum, herbaceous rhizomes, in the family Liliaceae/Melanthiaceae, all native to the temperate regions of the northern hemisphere.

Veratrum album
Origin: Europe, Siberia
Height: 5ft/1.5m
Z: 4

&❧ The false helleborine is a dazzling and exotic European native. The leaves are the first sign that this is something special. They unfold from the ground in April, a brilliant fresh green, curved and crisply pleated, 12in/30cm long and wonderfully ornamental. From these leaves a spire of flowers opens in June, each 1in/2.5cm across, a creamy green. This stately herbaceous plant has great presence in a border. *Veratrum nigrum* is very similar in all respects except that its flowers are a dramatic very deep purple. They may both be propagated by division.

Zephyranthes

There are about seventy species of zephyranthes, in the family Liliaceae/Amaryllidaceae, all bulbous plants native to the Americas.

Zephyranthes candida
Origin: South America
Height: 8in/20cm
Z: 8

&❧ This jaunty little bulb performs brilliantly in August when few other bulbous plants are in action. Single white flowers, 2in/5cm across, have delicately ribbed petals and prominent yellow stamens and are carried at the tips of pale green rush-like stems. It must have a very warm and sunny position and will not survive a cold damp site. It may be propagated by seed.

HERBACEOUS PERENNIALS

❧

Herbaceous plants are the indispensable part-timers of the garden. Many form no permanent top growth and, at the season's end, retreat into the ground to conserve their energies for their rebirth the following year. They are the most flexible of plants, generally easy to propagate and to move to a new site, allowing experiments and the swift correction of mistakes.

Herbaceous plants provide a long and colourful flowering season and valuable ornamental foliage. Their youthful growth, nosing through the soil among the spring bulbs, is always an exciting moment in the gardening year. As the foliage unfurls they very quickly begin to make a contribution to the whole appearance of the border: the marvellous structural leaves of acanthus or cardoons, for example; or the richness of peony stems and foliage culminating later on in dramatic flowers. Others, less spectacular, make their contribution in a more tentative way: cranesbills or *Viola cornuta*, for example, will scramble through other plants, providing subtle splashes of colour and forming happy associations with the plants with which they intermingle.

Although the sunny border is the place most easily associated with the floriferous display of herbaceous plants, others perform brilliantly in the shade. Ferns, hellebores and pulmonarias will make a fine show in places that other plants

would shun. An old-fashioned herbaceous border –
restricted to herbaceous plants only – is a grand sight in
summer, but it is extremely labour intensive and since
the plants provide no year-round ornament or shape, it
limits the scope of the smaller garden. By far the most
valuable use of herbaceous plants is in the mixed
border, where they add colour, drama and variety to
those woody plants that give all-season structure to the
garden.

Acanthus

There are thirty species of acanthus, all herbaceous,
in the family Acanthaceae and most are native to
Asia Minor and southern Europe.

Acanthus spinosus

Acanthus hirsutus
Origin: Turkey
Height: 24in/60cm
Z: 8

❧ This unusual Turkish acanthus has much of the
character of the more commonly seen *A. spinosus*
described below, but on a smaller scale and with subtle
variations. The leaves are much narrower, 12in/30cm
long, with pointed lobes. The flowers, in June or July,
are 24in/60cm long brush-like heads of cream and pale
green, an exquisite combination. It is best in heavy, rich
soil and must have a sunny position. In the border it
has emphatic shape and is wonderful in harmony with
yellows and pale blues. It sometimes sets seed and it
may also be propagated by division.

Acanthus spinosus
Origin: S. Europe
Height: $3^{1}/_{2}$ft/1m
Z: 6

ﻝ﮲ The great curved fronds of this acanthus, contrasting so handsomely with its curious vertical flowers, give it unique character. The leaves which unfold during April and May are up to 36in/90cm long, glistening dark green and intricately cut into deep pointed lobes. From this spectacular mound of foliage long flowering heads emerge in June or July, bold stems bearing many hooded flowers coloured cream and purple-pink, lasting for several weeks. It is a big bold border plant of great architectural character; a clump marking each end of a border looks very handsome. It will grow well in poor soil and in sun or semi-shade. In richer conditions it can be invasive, spreading by its fleshy roots. It may be propagated by seed or by division.

Achillea

There are eighty-five species of achillea, all herbaceous, in the family Compositae, and native to the temperate parts of the northern hemisphere.

Achillea clypeolata
Origin: E. Europe
Height: 30in/75cm
Z: 6

ﻝ﮲ The fern-like silvery foliage of this achillea is wonderfully elegant and ornamental. The leaves are twisting, narrow, pinnate, up to 12in/30cm long, each leaflet delicately lobed. In June the flowers are carried on tall stems, flat heads 4in/10cm across, of infinitesimally small yellow flowers. An especially good hybrid, with the same beautiful foliage as the type, is 'Moonshine' with fine lemon-yellow flowers.

This is an essential plant for borders with an emphasis on white/cream/yellow but it also looks beautiful with rich violet irises. It enjoys a sunny position in rich moist soil.

Agapanthus

There are ten species of agapanthus, in the family Liliaceae/Alliaceae, all of which are native to South Africa. There are some very beautiful species agapanthus which are not hardy in any but the most favoured gardens. Those described below are all beautiful and reasonably hardy but they must have a sunny position and will flower best in rich but well-drained soil. They may be propagated by division. Flowering in late summer they provide some of the most beautiful border plants of the season. They must be planted in bold clumps; dotty planting looks ridiculous.

Agapanthus Headbourne hybrid

Agapanthus Headbourne
hybrids
Origin: Garden
Height: 24–60in/
60cm–150cm
Z: 7

❧ Derived from *A. campanulatus*, these hybrids are the most widely seen agapanthus in gardens. They have been selected for their hardiness and the excellence of their colours, which range from the very palest to the darkest blue. All have superb loosely spherical heads of little trumpet flowers up to 6in/15cm across and about 1in/2.5cm long, the blue ones a delicate silvery blue within. The flowers, starting in July, are borne on swaying stems high above very decorative evergreen foliage, glistening and strap-like, arranged in bold sheaves. There are many unnamed varieties but two especially good ones are 'Ben Hope' which is up to 36in/90cm tall, with striking glaucous foliage, and flowers of a handsome grey-blue; and 'Loch Hope', a superb tall variety (to 5ft/1.5m) with deep blue flowers, not flowering until August.

Alchemilla

A genus of about thirty species of herbaceous perennials in the family Rosaceae, native to North America, Europe and Asia.

Alchemilla mollis
Origin: Asia Minor
Height: 18in/45cm
Z: 4

❧ Lady's mantle, common and easy, is an essential and decorative garden plant. Its leaves unfold in April – rounded, pleated, suede-soft and lime-green; they readily hold drops of water, rain or dew, which sparkle on the surface. Spires of diminutive straw-yellow

flowers open in May and last throughout the summer.
These should be removed in all but the wildest garden
because it is a prolific self-seeder; clip them off as soon
as they show signs of going brown in late summer.
Lady's mantle will do well in almost any position and
its colours consort harmoniously with many garden
arrangements. Cream, white or yellow tulips look
marvellous against its foliage, and later in the season it
looks well in a border with the soft blues of
campanulas and the orange of crocosmia.

Anemone

There are about seventy species of anemone, in the
family Ranunculaceae, herbaceous perennials with
tuberous (see page 15) or fibrous root-stock. They are
widely distributed in the temperate regions of both
hemispheres.

Anemone × hybrida
Origin: Garden
Height: 5ft/1.5m
Z: 5

❧ The so-called Japanese anemones are a magnificent
late summer ornament of the garden. The foliage is
very handsome: bold palm-shaped leaves with pointed
lobes, up to 6in/15cm long. The flowers are carried
high above on slender purple stems. The spherical buds
plump up in June and are at first silver then, just before

opening in July, a startling red. The flowers, borne for many weeks, are single, up to 3in/8cm across, a warm rosy pink, delicately veined, with an emphatic bush of golden stamens. Sometimes difficult to establish (and equally hard to eradicate!), it is at its most vigorous in rich heavy soil where it may become invasive. It will flower well in part shade or sun. I grow it surrounding a large bush of *Hydrangea aspera villosa* among whose lower branches the anemone decoratively interweaves. It is one of the great border plants, getting into full splendid stride as midsummer plantings are flagging. There is a glowing white form, *A. × h.* 'Honorine Jobert', every bit as beautiful as her pink sister. They may be propagated all too easily by root division.

Anthemis

Anthemis tinctoria
Origin: Europe
Height: 18in/45cm
Z: 4

There are about seventy species of this genus, in the family Compositae, whose native habitats are in Europe, Asia and north Africa.

❧ The yellow chamomile is a northern European native which has produced a garden variety, *A.t.* 'E.C. Buxton', which is an essential border plant. Its evergreen foliage makes a mound of fern-like mid-green leaves above which single flowers are borne constantly from June to the first frosts; they are a soft creamy yellow, 2in/5cm across, and consort admirably

with other flowering plants. I have it near pale blue-flowered *Campanula persicifolia*. It has no special requirements as to soil but it should be cut back hard after flowering to stimulate growth from the base. This new growth provides excellent material for cuttings.

Aquilegia vulgaris

Aquilegia

There are about seventy species of aquilegia, in the family Ranunculaceae, all from the temperate regions of the northern hemisphere except for one or two from South Africa.

Aquilegia canadensis
Origin: E. North America
Height: 18in/45cm
Z: 4

❧ This little North American columbine is a charming and cheerful plant which will naturalize uninvasively in appropriate conditions. The foliage is dark green, rounded and lobed, and the flowers appear in May, several on each stem. They are 1in/2.5cm across, with a straight spur behind, red above and lemon-yellow lower down. It likes a sunny position and rich soil where it will seed itself freely. It will weave through other plants and it is ideal for a border with a 'hot' colour scheme.

Aquilegia vulgaris
Origin: Europe
Height: 30in/75cm
Z: 5

❧ The wild European columbine is the sort of decorative plant which readily establishes itself in the garden, seeding freely and producing flowers of different colours. The foliage is extremely ornamental – glaucous-green, three-part, rounded and lobed, 2¹/₂in/6cm across. The flowers appear in May, borne high on slender stems, like elaborate pleated and winged hats, up to 2¹/₂in/6cm across and varying in colour from pinkish-violet to deep purple. Natural variations occur and white and blue flowers may be produced. 'Nora Barlow' has almost spherical flowers with ivory-white and red petals. All are beautiful and this charming border plant of early summer intermingles attractively with other plants. It will grow well in semi-shade or sun.

Artemisia

There are over 400 species, woody and herbaceous, in this genus, in the family Compositae, whose natural habitat is in the northern hemisphere and South America. For woody species see page 167.

Artemisia ludoviciana latiloba
Origin: North America
Height: 18in/45cm
Z: 4

❧ The foliage is the thing with this valuable plant. The leaves emerge in April, 3in/8cm long, a pale silvery grey with deeply jagged edges, carried in elegant plumes. It spreads by running roots, but not uncontrollably so and intermingles with other plants in the border,

Artemisia ludoviciana latiloba intermingled with *Geranium endressii*

providing both an admirable background as well as foliage interest in its own right. It is particularly beautiful with shades of red and purple. It performs at its best in a sunny or semi-shaded place and will have the palest colour in poor stony soil. It is easy to propagate by chopping off a part of the roots at almost any time of the year.

Asarum

There are about seventy species of asarum, all herbaceous, in the family Aristolochiaceae, native to North America, east Asia and Europe.

Asarum europaeum
Origin: Europe:
Height: 6in/15cm
Z: 4

❧ This shade-loving spreading plant has shining, handsomely shaped leaves that flourish in the shade. Each leaf is like a rounded heart, up to 4in/10cm wide by 2in/5cm long, very deep glossy green and delicately veined in a paler colour. The little brown flowers in spring, almost invisible, are of no account. Most authorities say that it is for a damp site. I grow it very successfully in that most difficult position, dry shade, where it brings a beautiful flash of light to a group of ferns and pulmonarias. It is shallow-rooted and spreads gently, making a good underplanting for shade-loving shrubs. It may be propagated by division.

Asplenium

Asplenium scolopendrium
(Phyllitis scolopendrium)
Origin: North America,
Asia, Europe
Height: 12in/30cm
Z: 4

There are two species of asplenium in the Aspleniaceae, one of the several families of ferns.

❧ The hart's tongue fern, a lovely ornament of wild hedgerows and the fringes of woodland, is a marvellous garden plant. In late April its fascinating leaves begin to unroll, elegantly curved like the neck of a violin, becoming shining narrow straps of lively green, 18in/45cm long and 2in/5cm wide. It flourishes in dry places, including shade, to which it brings rare distinction. A variety called *A.s.* 'Crispa' has especially decorative ruffled edges to the leaves and another, *A.s.* 'Golden Queen', is the same but a handsome golden-yellow.

Aster

Aster × frikartii 'Mönch'
Origin: Garden
Height: 36in/90cm
Z: 5

Aster novi-belgii
Origin: N.E. North America
Height: 3–6ft/1–1.8m
Z: 4

There are about 250 species of aster, in the family Compositae, all herbaceous perennials native to Africa, South America, Asia and Europe.

❧ This late-flowering hybrid gives wonderful ornament from July through to the autumn. The flowers are 2¹/₂in/6cm across, single but with many well-separated petals. The colour is a pale but emphatic lavender-blue, set off by a plump yellow centre. It is self-supporting in all but the most exposed places and produces its flowers with abandon. It must have an open position and plenty of nourishment and it may be propagated by division.

❧ The Michaelmas daisy, flowering in September and October, is a splendidly old-fashioned plant. It is known in a huge number of cultivars with single or very double daisy flowers in white, pink, red or blue and intermediate shades. There is no point in naming cultivars; the important matter is to choose the colour and size appropriate to your scheme. For the best effect it must be planted in substantial drifts. It must have fertile soil and a sunny position and will need to be divided every three or four years.

Astrantia

There are about five species of astrantia, in the family Umbelliferae, native to Asia and Europe.

Astrantia major
Origin: Europe
Height: 24in/60cm
Z: 4

❧ The decorative leaves of this astrantia, emerging in April, are variable, but all are in five parts, up to 6in/15cm across, and more, or less, finely cut. The flowers are unlike any other: ghostly grey many-pointed stars, veined and tipped with green, 1in/2.5cm across. With its distinctive foliage and mysteriously beautiful flowers it is a valuable border plant, adding charm to any planting. An especially striking cultivar, *A.m. involucrata* 'Shaggy', has much larger flowers than the type. It flourishes in semi-shade or sun, doing especially well in moist soil, and self-seeds with abandon. *A.m.i.* 'Shaggy' is not certain to come true by seed and the only reliable way to propagate is by division in autumn.

Baptisia

Baptisia australis
Origin: E. North America
Height: 4ft/1.2m
Z: 5

There are about seventeen species of baptisia, in the family Leguminosae, all herbaceous plants native to eastern North America.

❧ The leaves of this understated but beautiful plant emerge in April, at first pale grey they unfold to become soft glaucous-green, 2in/5cm long, narrow, rounded, pointed and carried on ghostly pale stems. The spires of pea flowers in June are rich violet-blue, 1in/2.5cm long, giving the whole plant the appearance of a colour arrangement by some discreet but masterly couturier. Long after the flowers have faded the foliage will continue to ornament the border. It likes moist soil, not too alkaline, in a sunny or semi-shade position, and it may be propagated by division.

Bergenia

Bergenia stracheyi

There are eight species of bergenia, evergreen herbaceous perennials in the family Saxifragaceae, native to east Asia. Although providing winter ornament, both in flower and in foliage, some are coarse and weed-like. Both those described below may be propagated by division.

Bergenia purpurascens
Origin: Himalaya
Height: 18in/45cm
Z: 4

❧ The bold but narrow leaves of this bergenia, up to 7in/18cm long, colour a shade of deep bruised red in winter. The flowers in March are generous sprawling panicles of pink-red. I have seen it excellently used to form an informal edging to a border with a red and purple colour scheme. It will do well in a moist site in part shade.

Bergenia stracheyi
Origin: Asia
Height: 12in/30cm
Z: 6

❧ The rounded leaves, up to 6in/10cm across, will turn a rich wine-red in cold weather. The flowers, delicate clusters of miniature bells, appear in March, very pale pink and sweetly scented. It has an air of true distinction to it and is a valuable ornament for part shade where it looks beautiful with hellebores and pale blue pulmonarias. There is a particularly fine white form, *B.s. alba*.

Briza

There are twelve species of briza, in the family Gramineae, widely distributed in northern temperate regions.

Briza media
Origin: Asia, Europe
Height: 18in/45cm
Z: 5

❧ The beautiful thing about this perennial grass is the feature that gives it its common name of quaking grass. The seed heads, intricately fashioned like lockets with overlapping plates, perpetually sway at the downward pointing tips of very fine curved purple stems. They are russet brown, $^1/_2$in/1.25cm long, and are formed in June, after which they will remain throughout the season. This is an elegant plant which may certainly find its decorative place in the border where it will do best in a sunny position. It may be propagated by division or by seed.

Brunnera

A genus of three species in the family Boraginaceae, native to the eastern Mediterranean.

Brunnera macrophylla
Origin: W. Caucasus
Height: 18in/45cm
Z: 4

❧ In March or April the cheerful forget-me-not blue and pale eye of the diminutive flowers, held above downy heart-shaped foliage, is one of the earliest herbaceous delights of the season. The plant does well in shade (even quite dry shade), and is a valuable ground-cover. It is very easy to propagate by root division in late autumn. *B. m.* 'Hadspen Cream' is a particularly distinguished form with foliage of handsome creamy variegations.

Campanula

There are about 300 species of campanula, in the family Campanulaceae, widely distributed in the temperate regions of the northern hemisphere. They are the delight of alpine plant specialists and a few are absolutely essential border plants.

Campanula lactiflora
Origin: Caucasus
Height: 5ft/1.5m
Z: 4

❧ This is among the tallest and most strikingly handsome of the campanulas. The leaves are pointed and toothed, 3in/8cm long. The flowers in June are borne on tall stems, each trumpet-shaped with outward-pointing pointed petals, clear blue-purple, carried very profusely. It is very tough and is valuable in the mixed border where it has the presence to consort with substantial shrubs, especially those with pale foliage such as *Elaeagnus commutata*. There is a beautiful white form, *C.l. alba*, and a good pale pink variety, *C.l.* 'Loddon Anna'.

Campanula latiloba
Origin: Siberia
Height: 36in/90cm
Z: 3

❧ Profusely covered flowering stems erupt from rosettes of leaves in this spectacular campanula. Each flower is single, cupped, but opening widely, 2in/5cm across, an excellent clear blue. There is also a fine white form, *C.l. alba*, of exceptional delicacy, which looks lovely in the border with creams and pale yellows such as *Anthemis tinctoria* 'E.C. Buxton'. It will do well in semi-shade and may be propagated by division.

Campanula persicifolia

Campanula persicifolia
Origin: N. Africa, Asia, Europe
Height: 36in/90cm
Z: 3

❧ In June the flowers of this tall campanula are a marvellous sight. They are single bells, carried along the stems, 2¹/₂/5cm across, a clear violet-blue. The leaves are slender, pointed and 4in/10cm long. There is a good white-flowered form, *C.p. alba*, and a dazzling fully double version of it, *C.p.* 'Alba Flore Pleno'. Because the plants are slender and the flowers borne high this is an excellent plant for the crowded border. It will flower well in semi-shade as well as in sun, and enjoys rich heavy soil. It may be propagated by division or seed.

Campanula takesimana
Origin: Korea
Height: 18in/45cm
Z: 5

❧ The leaves of this campanula are boldly heart-shaped, up to 4in/10cm long, and some of them have margins flushed with brownish-red. The flowers in July or August are striking tubes 2¹/₂in/6cm long, pale pink-mauve and speckled inside with raspberry-coloured spots. Heavy moist soil suits it well, where its creeping roots may become embarrassingly invasive; it will flourish in a position in part shade. Plant it in a densely packed border where neighbouring plants may support it. It may be propagated by division.

Centaurea

There are about 450 species of centaurea, in the family Compositae, native to America, Asia, Australia and the Mediterranean countries.

Centaurea 'Pulchra Major'
Origin: Garden
Height: 24in/60cm
Z: 7

Centranthus

Centranthus ruber
Origin: Asia Minor, Europe
Height: 36in/90cm
Z: 5

Cheiranthus

☙ At a careless glance this could be seen as a weed but the more carefully it is scrutinized the more obvious its distinction becomes. Its leaves are a lovely glaucous-green, with pointed upward-pointing lobes, about 4in/10cm long. The 2½in/6cm flowers, opening in June, are exquisitely beautiful, thistle-like in shape with a profusion of very fine clear mauve-pink petals erupting from the top. The lower half of the head is covered in intricate overlapping scales, like the feathers of some very small bird, a lovely pale gold colour. It must have a sunny position and well-drained soil. It will give much pleasure towards the front of the border, and the flower heads remain very ornamental long after they have browned. It may be propagated by division or seed.

There are about twelve species of centranthus, in the family Valerianaceae, native to Europe and the Mediterranean countries.

☙ In some circumstances, in the crevices of old walls for example, valerian can become an embarrassingly invasive plant, but it has a stately beauty. The stems and leaves are glaucous-grey, each leaf up to 3in/8cm long, curvaceous and pointed. The flowers in May or June are very small but held in generous plumes. They vary in colour from a rather insipid mauve-pink to a handsome clear red. *C.r. albus* is white and makes a marvellous and harmonious plant for repeat planting in the border, looking especially good at the feet of shrub roses and consorting easily with any colour scheme. It is best in a sunny position but will thrive in even the poorest soil. By weeding out undesirable seedlings you may establish a self-perpetuating colony of the colour you want.

There are about ten species of cheiranthus in the family Cruciferae, native to the temperate regions of the northern hemisphere.

Cheiranthus cheiri
Origin: S.E. Europe
Height: 12in/30cm
Z: 7

❧ The wild European wallflower has given rise to admirable garden varieties, all evergreen with narrow mid-green leaves. *C.c.* 'Bloody Warrior', an old cultivar, has spires of rich crimson flowers; *C.c.* 'Harpur Crewe' has spires of little egg-yolk yellow flowers. In both cases the flowers are borne from April onwards over a long flowering season. They have the delicious, distinctive wallflower scent, sweet and slightly musky. They have no special soil needs but will flower best in a sunny position. They are not long-lived but may be propagated very easily by taking cuttings from the slightly woody old growth.

Clematis

There are about 250 species of clematis, in the family Ranunculaceae, very widely distributed in every continent in the world. Most of the species are woody climbers (see pages 239–44) but that described below is herbaceous.

Clematis × durandii
Origin: Garden
Height: 6ft/1.8m
Z: 5

❧ This hybrid between a herbaceous and a woody clematis has produced an outstandingly beautiful plant. The foliage is boldly heart-shaped, slightly toothed and up to 3in/8cm long. The flowers, opening in June but lasting for a very long season, are 4in/10cm across, single, an intense violet-blue that gradually fades to

silver-blue. In the border it will intermingle with other plants; it looks especially beautiful supported by the silver-leaved *Elaeagnus commutata*. It may be propagated by cuttings or division.

Convolvulus

There are about 250 species of convolvulus, herbaceous and woody, in the family Convolvulaceae, very widely distributed. They include the lovely but alarming European bindweed, *Convolvulus arvensis*, which only the boldest gardener would introduce into the garden. See also page 178 in the section on shrubs.

Convolvulus althaeoïdes
Origin: S. Europe
Height: 12in/30cm
Z: 8

❧ In conditions that suit it this beautiful twining plant may become invasive; however, it is so decorative that some way of accommodating it should be found – if necessary in a container. It comes to life late in the season, leaves breaking through the soil in May. The grey foliage is curious: the twining tendrils have very narrow leaves, 1½in/4cm long, but those at the base

91

are lobed like an oak leaf, 2in/5cm long. The funnel-shaped flowers in June and throughout the growing season are single, a clear silvery pink, 1¹/₂in/4cm across. It is wonderful growing throughout more substantial plants where it will easily rise 4–5ft/1.2–1.5m. I grow it through the variegated foliage of *Cornus alternifolia* 'Argentea'. It must have a sunny position in light soil. It may be propagated by division.

Convolvulus sabatius
(*C. mauretanicus*)
Origin: Mediterranean
Height: 6in/15cm
Z: 8

❧ The foliage of this creeping plant is rounded, a lovely silvery grey, 1in/2.5cm across; the flowers, starting in June but continuing for many weeks, are a rich blue-purple with a pale eye, 1¹/₂in/3cm across. It must have a sunny position but seems to like a moist root run. I have grown it, almost too successfully, between flagstones. At all events, this is not a border plant but a lovely decoration for some odd corner. It may be propagated by division.

Coreopsis

There are about eighty species of coreopsis, in the family Compositae, all herbaceous plants native to Central, North and South America.

Coreopsis lanceolata
Origin: Central and
S.E. North America
Height: 24in/60cm
Z: 4

❧ This daisy-like perennial produces its flowers throughout the season. The leaves are slender and pointed, 3in/8cm long, mid-green and slightly marbled. The flowers, opening in June from plump spherical purple-tipped buds, are semi-double, 2in/5cm across, a rich shade of yellow becoming darker towards the centre, with a very pronounced mound of anthers. The tips of each petal are jagged, giving the whole flower a lively edge. This is not a plant for gardeners who shrink from bold colours but in a border of hot colours it is extremely ornamental. It will flower best in a sunny position with rich soil. It is not long-lived and may be propagated by seed or division. There are many cultivars, of varying shades of yellow and some with brown eyes or splashes, but such elaborations only detract from the straightforward brilliance and charm of the type.

Cynara

There are ten species of cynara, all herbaceous, in the family Compositae, native to the Mediterranean countries and the Canary Islands.

Cynara cardunculus
Origin: Mediterranean
Height: 7ft/2m
Z: 6

❧ The cardoon produces among the most spectacular and beautiful foliage of any plant. The leaves, fully unfurled by late May or June, are great curving fronds, up to 4ft/1.2m long, a marvellous silvery grey and elegantly cut into pointed lobes. The prickly purple

93

Illustration opposite:
Delphinium 'Lord Butler'

flowers in June, 4in/10cm across, are carried on tall stiff stems, and still highly decorative when brown and dry in the autumn. This bold architectural plant gives powerful structure to the border and makes a wonderful background to other plantings. It needs a sunny position and generous feeding. It may be propagated by division.

Delphinium

There are about 250 species of delphinium, all herbaceous, in the family Ranunculaceae, native to the temperate regions of the northern hemisphere.

Delphinium cultivars
Origin: Garden
Height: 8ft/2.5m
Z: 3

❧ The very tall border delphinium was first seen in gardens just over 100 years ago. The foliage is very handsome: deeply cut fronds, up to 12in/30cm across, of a striking glaucous-green. The flowers, opening in June, are typically 2–2$^{1}/_{2}$in/5–6cm across, semi-double, often with frilly margins and ranging in colour from white, mauve, purple, to deep blue. Some have a very attractive contrasting 'eye' at the centre of each flower. Cultivar names come and go with bewildering speed so there is little point in recommending particular varieties. They need rich soil (a good mulch of humus as the plants emerge in spring is beneficial) and flower best in a sunny open position. They need staking and flower spikes should be cut off after flowering (leaving a short stem to provide seed if you want to preserve it). They must be propagated by division or cuttings to preserve their identity.

Delphinium tatsienense

The shorter Belladonna hybrids (up to 5ft/1.5m), with decorative spurred flowers in shades of blue and a very long flowering season, are valuable for the smaller garden. In a densely planted border the shorter kinds may be supported by surrounding plantings. They have exactly the same cultivation needs as the taller kinds.

Delphinium tatsienense
Origin: China
Height: 18in/45cm
Z: 7

❧ This little delphinium has dazzling rich blue flowers, and although short-lived, in favourable circumstances it will seed itself. The leaves are very deeply cut, a lively green, 3in/8cm across. The flowers,

borne in June, an intense, piercing blue, are no more than 3/4in/2cm long, carried at the end of thin stems. It likes a very sunny dry position and is beautiful with smaller grey-leaved shrubs such as artemisias and santolinas. There is a white-flowered form, *D.t. album,* which seems to defeat the whole point of the plant.

Dianthus

There are about 300 species of dianthus, which include carnations, pinks and sweet williams, in the family Caryophyllaceae, virtually all native to the Mediterranean countries and west Asia. The smaller species, very suitable for troughs and rockeries, are not sufficiently substantial or easy enough to cultivate for everyday decorative life in the garden.

Dianthus cultivars
Origin: Garden
Height: 4–9in/10–22.5cm
Z: 3

❧ Garden pinks are very variable, hybridizing freely, and they provide some of the most attractive and useful smaller plants for the edges of borders. The foliage is grass-like, a decorative pale glaucous-grey, and the flowers are borne aloft from June onwards, 1in/2.5cm across and varying in colour – white, pink, mauve and deep red, and often combinations of these, best of all splashed or ringed with contrasting colour. Most are deliciously scented – one of the essential perfumes of the summer garden. They must have a sunny site that is well drained but even here they are short-lived, and in

any case flower best when young. They may be propagated by seed, flowering the following year. Especially good forms may be propagated by cuttings.

Diascia rigescens

Diascia

Diascia rigescens
Origin: South Africa
Height: 18in/45cm
Z: 8

There are about fifty species of diascia, in the family Scrophulariaceae, native to South Africa.

❧ Diascias are tender in all but the most favoured gardens but they are well worth taking trouble with. From clumps of insignificant leaves (which turn brown with age) upright spires, up to 18in/45cm tall, carry small tubular flowers like miniature fatter foxgloves, of a wonderful faded but striking russet-pink unlike any other flower. It must have well-drained soil in a sunny position; the top of a low wall suits it well and allows it to flop over decoratively. It may be propagated by cuttings. There are cultivars but none that I have seen is better than the type.

Dicentra

There are about a dozen species of dicentra, in the family Fumariaceae, native to North America and eastern Asia.

Dicentra formosa
Origin: North America
Height: 18in/45cm
Z: 4

🐛 This has among the most beautiful foliage of any herbaceous plant. It emerges in March, very finely cut and fern-like, a beguiling glaucous-grey. The flowers appear in April and are carried on slender pink stems, curious hanging pouches of pink-mauve. An especially good cultivar is *D.f.* 'Stuart Boothman' with even more finely cut leaves, edged with a hint of pink, and flowers of a rich carmine-pink. Another cultivar, of uncertain parentage, 'Bacchanal' has deep blood-red flowers of exceptional distinction. All these prefer a position in semi-shade, and in rich soil will spread vigorously. They are effortlessly propagated by chopping off a piece of fleshy root at almost any time. After flowering the foliage continues to be ornamental throughout the season, making an excellent background in the border for later flowering plants such as trailing herbaceous potentillas.

Dicentra formosa 'Stuart Boothman'

Dicentra spectabilis
Origin: Japan, Siberia
Height: 24in/60cm
Z: 3

🐛 Dutchman's breeches (which the flowers are said to resemble) makes a bold clump of pale lime-green slightly toothed leaves. The flowers appear in April, dangling below arching stems, pink and rose heart-shaped pouches which, to my taste, are a little over the top – a bit like cheap sweets. But there is a white form, *D.s. alba,* which is a wonderful border plant, flourishing in part shade or in sun, and consorting obligingly with any colour scheme. As part of a white, yellow and grey arrangement its lime-green foliage and white flowers are seen to excellent effect. It is easy to propagate by division.

Dicentra spectabilis alba

Dictamnus

Dictamnus albus
Origin: Europe to E. Asia
Height: 36in/90cm
Z: 3

There is only one species of dictamnus, in the family Rutaceae, and native to a very wide area from Europe to Japan.

❧ The common name for dictamnus is burning bush, because of the inflammable oils which it gives off in warm weather. It is an exceptionally stately plant for the border, distinguished in foliage and flower. The leaves are pinnate, each leaflet 1½in/4cm long, and the flowers, opening in May or June, are carried in striking spires, up to 18in/45cm long. Each flower is an elegant little white trumpet, opening wide in the sun. An especially attractive form is *D.a.* 'Purpureus' whose flowers vary in colour from reddish-pink to light purple, attractively veined in a deeper shade. It likes rich soil and will perform equally well in sun or part shade. It may be propagated by seed but plants will be slow to flower and it is best to propagate by division.

Dictamnus albus
'Purpureus'

Epilobium

Epilobium angustifolium leucanthum (E.a. album)
Origin: N. hemisphere
Height: 6ft/1.8m
Z: 3

There are about 200 species of epilobium, in the family Onagraceae, very widely distributed in temperate regions.

❧ Some gardeners find this too much like a weed to introduce safely into the garden but Gertrude Jekyll liked it and so do I. It has soft grey-green narrow pointed leaves, up to 5in/13cm long, and from June onwards the stems are crowned with many single white flowers, 1in/2.5cm across, with the faintest flush of pink. In rich moist soil it is very invasive. I grow it in dry shade in rather poor soil where it glows decoratively in the gloom and loses some of its imperialistic tendencies. It is, of course, effortlessly propagated by division or by seed.

Epimedium

There are about twenty species of epimedium in the family Berberidaceae, native to the Caucasus, Europe, Japan and North Africa.

Epimedium grandiflorum
Origin: Japan
Height: 16in/40cm
Z: 5

❧ This very ornamental plant is sometimes belittled by being considered merely as useful ground-cover. It is evergreen with leaves shaped like slender hearts, 4in/10cm long when mature, and edged and dappled with bronze-red; the new foliage is much smaller and a pale lime-green. Flowers from April onwards are carried airily on slender stems, resembling diminutive aquilegias and varying in colour from pale lemon-yellow to pink and blue-purple. *E.g.* 'Rose Queen' is a striking cultivar with rich red flowers tipped with white. It will flourish in the most inhospitable places including dry poor soil in dense shade. It is easily propagated by root division at almost any time.

Erigeron

There are well over 150 species of erigeron, in the family Compositae, very widely distributed in the temperate regions.

Erigeron karvinskianus
(E. mucronatus)
Origin: Mexico
Height: 9in/22.5cm
Z: 7

❧ This little evergreen Mexican daisy is supposedly tender and needs a site in full sun. I grow it in crevices at the foot of a north-facing wall where it flowers profusely and self-seeds obligingly. It starts to flower in May and continues throughout the season until the first frosts. The flowers are many-petalled, 3/4in/2cm across, white changing to warm pink, with emphatic lime-green stamens. The slender slightly lobed leaves, 1 1/2in/4cm long, are a lively mid-green. It will seed itself in places with apparently no nourishment; it is supremely the plant for odd corners – between flagstones, festooning a dry-stone wall or fringing steps.

Illustration opposite:
Erigeron karvinskianus

Eryngium

There are over 200 species of eryngium, in the family Umbelliferae, widely distributed, with some from tropical South America; most are of a decorative thistle-like character.

Eryngium alpinum
Origin: Europe
Height: 24in/60cm
Z: 5

❧ The striking cone-like flowers of this sea-holly, opening in June, are fringed with spreading metallic-blue bracts of extraordinary elaboration and delicacy. They are borne on blue stems which rise from clumps of glistening heart-shaped foliage. It must have

sun but will flourish in poor soil. In the border it has a special affinity with soft silver pinks and looks wonderful, for example, with *Cistus × purpureus*. It may be propagated by seed or division.

Eryngium bourgatii
Origin: Spain
Height: 18in/45cm
Z: 5

❧ This little sea-holly, with intricate deeply cut spiny foliage, is a continuously decorative garden plant. It forms an upright clump and the leaves, 6in/15cm long, are a metallic grey-green finely mottled and veined in silver. The flowers, carried on slender branching stems in June, silvery violet thistle spheres 1 1/2in/4cm across, last throughout the season and remain decorative when dead. For the front of the border, in a sunny well-drained place, this is a lovely plant. It may be propagated by seed or by division.

Eryngium bourgatii

Eryngium giganteum
Origin: Caucasus
Height: 24in/60cm
Z: 6

❧ This lovely plant, known as Miss Willmott's Ghost, is a perennial but flowers only once and then dies. The leaves at the base are up to 6in/15cm long, triangular and sharply pointed, patterned with silver tracery. The flowers have a central dark head framed by intricately filigreed silver-white bracts of exquisite detail and delicacy. It seeds itself freely and an easily established colony will enliven odd corners and harmonize marvellously with other plantings in the border. It looks especially beautiful with silvery blues such as the flax, *Linum narbonense*, and with pale pinks. It needs a sunny position but does well in poor soil.

Eryngium giganteum

Euphorbia

This is a huge genus with over 2,000 species, in the family Euphorbiaceae, widely distributed in temperate and tropical regions.

Euphorbia characias
Origin: W. Mediterranean
Height: 3ft/1m
Z: 7

❧ The glaucous-green foliage of this spurge is outstandingly beautiful and clumps of it contribute shapely presence to the border, harmonizing well with any colour scheme. In March the flowers unfurl, great plump heads of diminutive lime-green bell-shaped flowers with a deep brown-purple eye. In late summer or early autumn, when they have turned brown and

105

yellow, these should be cut back to their base; the new stems appearing at their feet will form in turn lovely winter ornament, retaining droplets of water – rain or dew – to sit sparkling on the leaf surfaces. It will self-seed and plants should in any case be renewed every three or four years as their flower display diminishes. A subspecies, *E.c. wulfenii*, has exhilarating yellow flower heads but is otherwise virtually identical.

Euphorbia characias wulfenii

Euphorbia griffithii
Origin: W. Asia
Height: 24in/60cm
Z: 4

❧ The first sign of this plant is of asparagus-like shoots in March, nosing through the bare soil to become fleshy rhubarb-red stems from which a progression of mid-green leaves unfolds as the stem grows. In May, orange-brown flowers appear, a startling and festive colour. This plant is almost always seen in gardens in the variety 'Fireglow' which has more intense colouring than the type. It is not choosy as to soil and is alarmingly easy to propagate by chopping off a piece of the fleshy root in autumn or spring. In rich moist soil it may become dangerously invasive but it is a very beautiful invader. In the border it looks marvellous against the plummy foliage of *Cotinus coggygria* 'Royal Purple'.

Euphorbia myrsinites
Origin: S. Europe
Height: 6in/15cm
Z: 5

❧ This is a curious plant which I find extremely decorative. Its chief distinction is its foliage in the form of straggling 'tails', up to 12in/30cm long, composed of leaves densely disposed about a central stem. The colour is beautiful, a distinguished pale glaucous-grey. Insignificant little yellow flowers appear at the end of the 'tails' in spring. It must have a sunny position, does well in poor dry soil and is at its very best where it can hang over a wall or the edge of a pot; this encourages foliage of even greater length. It self-seeds in a restrained way and seed may easily be gathered in the summer for propagation.

Euphorbia myrsinites

Euphorbia polychroma
Origin: Europe
Height: 18in/45cm
Z: 4

❧ This is one of the earlier herbaceous plants to perform, and its shapely habit, colour and structure make it an excellent border plant. The flowers – or rather bracts surrounding the rather insignificant flowers – open in April, a warm green-yellow, 3in/8cm across and contrasting subtly with the lime-green foliage. It naturally forms a domed mound about 24in/60cm across and does well in part shade, bringing a brilliant glow. It may be propagated by division.

Festuca

There are about 300 species of festuca, in the family Gramineae, distributed throughout the world.

Festuca glauca
Origin: Europe
Height: 12in/30cm
Z: 5

❧ This blue-grey fescue provides decorative foliage for the front of the border or for edging a path. It forms rounded mounds of very fine grassy blades of delicate blue-tinted grey. In late June handsome seed heads of the palest gold rise above. It looks wonderful as a background to the flowers and foliage of old-fashioned pinks. It will grow in sun or semi-shade but needs to be divided regularly; old clumps become straggly and shapeless.

Galega

Galega x hartlandii
Origin: Garden
Height: 4ft/1.2m
Z: 4

There are about six species of galega, all herbaceous, in the family Leguminosae, native to Africa, Asia and Europe.

❧ This goat's rue has a jolly, slightly coarse charm that some fastidious gardeners would disdain, but I like it. It forms a vigorously upright bush (which will need supporting) and the leaves are a soft green, in threes, each leaflet 2in/5cm long. The flowers, in June or July, borne in bold racemes, are diminutive and pea-like, white and blue on the same head. There is an old cultivar, *G. × h.* 'Lady Wilson', with mauve-pink flowers, that looks marvellous in a border with a red and purple emphasis. It performs best in sun and will thrive in poor soil. It may be propagated by division.

Gaura

There are twenty-one species of gaura, all herbaceous, in the family Onagraceae, all native to North America.

Gaura lindheimeri
Origin: North America
Height: 36in/90cm
Z: 2

❧ Plants that take up little room in the border and provide a long season of flowers borne high above others are especially desirable. This gaura throws up tall stems carrying narrow leaves, up to 5in/13cm long, some of which are curiously marked with black spots as though splashed with ink. The flowers appear in June or July and continue throughout the growing season. They open from slender pink-flushed buds, single, white, 1in/2.5cm across, carried in curving spires which sway attractively above lower plantings. It forms woody stems which should be cut back in the winter after flowering. It needs a sunny position and may be propagated by division.

Geranium

There are about 300 species of hardy geraniums, or cranesbills, in the family Geraniaceae which also includes the tender pelargoniums – still often misleadingly also called geraniums. Almost all are herbaceous, both deciduous and evergreen. Their natural distribution is very wide in the temperate parts of North and South America, Asia, the southern hemisphere and Europe. They are extremely attractive border plants, in flower as well as in foliage, and many of the larger ones will scramble through other plants in a most accommodating way. Some make valuable ground-cover with foliage and flowers that are equally decorative. Most are easily propagated by division at almost any time of the year, or by seed.

Geranium clarkei
'Kashmir White'
Origin: Garden (Himalaya)
Height: 9in/23cm
Zone: 7

❧ The leaves of this Himalayan cranesbill are exceptionally elegant. They are palm-shaped, up to 6in/15cm across, with seven fingers each of which is slender and cut into deep pointed lobes intricately marked with paler veins. The flowers, starting in May, are single, 2in/5cm across, a ghostly grey-white in colour with a tracery of grey veins. The flowers are held well above the foliage, giving the whole plant an air of distinction. It spreads by running roots and should be divided regularly to ensure a supply of young plants which flower much more profusely than old woody specimens.

Geranium clarkei
'Kashmir White'

Geranium himalayense
'Plenum'
Origin: Garden
Height: 6in/15cm
Z: 4

❧ The leaves of this geranium are deeply cut and lobed, up to 4in/10cm across, with a soft texture and pronounced veins. The flowers are extremely decorative, double, 1in/2.5cm across, a lively purple-blue with a paler eye in which darker veining

stands out. They are carried on trailing stems which will straggle through other plants. It is an admirable front-of-the-border plant where it will do best in a sunny position. I grow it intermingling with the deep purple-leaved sage, *Salvia officinalis* 'Purpurascens'. It spreads naturally but not uncontrollably. To encourage vigorous and floriferous plants it should be divided every three or four years.

Geranium macrorrhizum
Origin: Europe
Height: 9in/23cm
Z: 4

❧ The term ground-cover, much less frequently used in gardening these days, used to refer to a not especially distinguished plant that had the virtue of smothering even less distinguished plants. This beautiful geranium was too easily thought of in this way. It has distinguished lobed and deeply cut leaves, slightly hairy and of very soft texture, up to 4in/10cm across, giving off a pungent catmint-like scent. The flowers in May are carried nobly above the foliage, rather small but of a fine pale pink and borne in very great profusion. The foliage turns a splendid cherry-red in autumn. It will

111

grow and flower well in shade; I grow it under a *Magnolia stellata* where it produces its first flowers at the same time as the last of the magnolia. There is a white form, *G.m.* 'Album', whose flowers are given a flush of pink by the red calyces.

Geranium pratense 'Mrs Kendall Clark'

Geranium pratense
Origin: W. Europe, Asia and Japan
Height: 24–48in/ 60–120cm
Z: 4

❧ The meadow cranesbill, found widely on the verges of fields and roads in northern Europe, shows many variations; some of the forms are excellent garden plants. All have handsome grey-green deeply cut leaves, 12cm/5in across, and bear their usually single flowers, of a cheerful violet-blue in the species, and about 1in/2.5cm across, on slender upright stems in May or June. In the border they need support, which may be provided by other plants through which they can climb. If cut back after the first flowering they will produce a useful second scattering of flowers in late

summer. *G.p.* 'Mrs Kendall Clark' has pale grey-blue, finely veined flowers of ghostly delicacy.
G.p. 'Striatum' is white, irregularly splashed with blue. There are several double-flowered cultivars:
G.p. 'Plenum Album' is chalk white; *G.p.* 'Plenum Caeruleum' has clear blue flowers, and *G.p.* 'Plenum Violaceum' has strikingly deep violet double flowers.

Geranium renardii

Geranium renardii
Origin: Caucasus
Height: 6in/15cm
Z: 6

❧ The suede-soft rounded foliage, $2^1/_2$in/6cm across, is wonderfully ornamental at the edge of the border. The flowers are produced in May or June, of a pale and distinguished grey suffused with blue-violet veins, $1^1/_2$in/4cm across. It is one of the very best of the smaller geraniums.

Geranium sanguineum striatum
Origin: Europe, Turkey
Height: 8in/20cm
Z: 5

❧ The neat habit, decorative foliage and beautiful colour of this smaller geranium make it especially ornamental. The leaves are $1^1/_2$in/4cm across, deeply divided into finger-like lobes. The flowers, opening in May or June but continuing throughout the growing season, are single, $1^1/_2$in/4cm across, of a lovely very pale silvery pink etched with fine darker veins.

113

Geranium wallichianum
Origin: Afghanistan,
Himalaya and Kashmir
Height: 8in/20cm
Z: 4

❧ The species *Geranium wallichianum* is scarcely ever seen; it is far better known in the beautiful cultivar 'Buxton's Variety'. Of sprawling habit, its leaves are 3in/8cm across, borne on pinkish stems, decoratively mottled and slightly felted, colouring red-brown about the edges in cold weather. Its flowers are single, 1½in/4cm across, of a fine, slightly violet blue, becoming a clearer blue in cool weather, with a circle of white at the centre. It begins to flower in July and continues giving marvellous ornament until far into autumn. It will throw out new growth of up to 36in/90cm in a season, spreading its beautiful flowers and leaves through neighbouring planting. It breeds true from seed.

Gillenia

There are two species of gillenia, in the family Rosaceae, both native to North America.

Gillenia trifoliata
Origin: N.E. North America
Height: 36in/90cm
Z: 4

❧ Gracefulness is the essential quality of this plant. The leaves, carried on wiry red stems and appearing in April or May, are slender, toothed and pointed, up to 3in/8cm long and carried in threes. The flowers open in June, pink buds expanding into white flowers, like elegant little insects in flight, no more than 1in/2.5cm long. The foliage colours to a very lively russet-red early in the autumn. It is excellent in a sunny border, especially one with pinks, reds and whites, but it needs to be alongside plants of similar elegance. It is best propagated by seed collected in late autumn.

Glaucium

There are about twenty-five species of glaucium, or horned poppy, all herbaceous, in the family Papaveraceae, and native to Africa, Asia and Europe.

Glaucium flavum
Origin: N. Africa, W. Asia, Europe
36in/90cm
Z: 7

❧ The horned poppy has a marvellous combination of lemon-yellow flowers and very decorative glaucous foliage. The leaves, borne on rather stiff silvery stems, are a curious shape, rounded but with pointed lobes, sometimes undulating margins, glaucous-grey in colour and rather hairy, 2in/5cm across. The flowers, from June onwards, are a dazzling clear yellow, single, with papery fine petals, 2in/5cm across and with a deeper yellow centre. It forms curious sickle-shaped seed capsules up to 12in/30cm long. It must have a sunny position and sharp drainage. It looks wonderful with rich purple-blue *Viola cornuta*. This is a short-lived perennial but it may be propagated easily by seed.

Gunnera

There are about fifty species of gunnera, in the family Gunneraceae, native to Africa, South America and Australasia.

Gunnera manicata
Origin: South America
Height: 6ft/1.8m
Z: 7

☙ Few gardens have the right setting for this immense plant, and those which do should make full use of it. It stirs to life in March when thick pale green stems emerge, patterned with rough brown hairs and carrying the pale green, intricately folded leaves. When fully grown these are up to 6ft/1.8m across, rounded and rough-textured, with fretted lobes and strongly marked veins. It must have moist soil and a protected site, and is usually planted at the water's edge where it may be seen splendidly reflected. Its beauty lies in its curious combination of grandiose size and intricate detail. It may be propagated by division.

Helenium

Helenium 'Moerheim Beauty'
Origin: Garden
Height: 4ft/1.2m
Z: 4

There are about forty species of helenium, all herbaceous, in the family Compositae, native to the Americas.

☙ This helenium is unique for the intense rust-red of its decorative flowers which, starting in June but continuing over a long season, are many-petalled, 2in/5cm across, and bending back from a prominent rounded pincushion of stamens. The leaves are narrow, up to 3in/8cm long, a fresh pale green. It is indispensable for bold fiery colour schemes of yellow and red, where it should be used in substantial masses and not dotted about. It must have a sunny position and is very easily propagated by division.

Helleborus

There are about twenty species of hellebore, in the family Ranunculaceae, native to Europe and Asia Minor. They are rare among herbaceous plants in that they are decorative in one way or another at absolutely any time of year.

Helleborus argutifolius
(*H. corsicus*)
Origin: Mediterranean
Height: 24in/60cm
Z: 7

❧ If I had to choose only half-a-dozen herbaceous plants for my garden this would be among them. It forms an upright clump with bold foliage composed of groups of three leaves, each 4–5in/10–12.5cm long, finely toothed, slightly curving, of a leathery mottled texture. The flowers, in winter but lasting a long time, are single creamy green cups, 2¹/₂in/5cm across, borne

117

generously on long sturdy stems. It is not particular as to soil and will flourish in a cool north-facing position. I grow it in such a place, together with erythroniums and cyclamen, above which it rises, the very picture of distinction. It will seed itself in a usefully uninvasive way.

Helleborus foetidus
Origin: Europe
Height: 36in/90cm
Z: 6

❧ Stinking hellebore is an unpromising name for a garden plant but everything else about it is beautiful. It has stately palm-like fronds of evergreen foliage, each leaflet 4in/10cm long, narrow, pointed, finely toothed and with a slight curve. The flowers in late winter or early spring are borne in generous trusses high above the foliage, hanging green-yellow cups with a red rim. In the wild it is a woodland plant, often on poor, thin, dry soil, so in the garden it will perform most handsomely in places impossible for most other plants. It may be propagated by seed. There are selected clones of which an especially fine example is 'Wester Flisk' which has stems strikingly flushed with wine-red; some, too, have foliage of a lovely silvery green.

Helleborus foetidus

Helleborus orientalis
Origin: Asia Minor
Height: 18in/45cm
Z: 4

❧ The evergreen Lenten lily makes very handsome palm-shaped leaves, slightly toothed, each leaflet 4in/10cm long. In late winter the flowers appear, hanging and slightly cupped, 2$^{1}/_{2}$in/5cm across, of immensely variable colour, ranging from pinkish-white to a wonderful deep velvety purple. Some of the paler

colours are beautifully splashed with raspberry-coloured spots within. It is at its best in semi- or complete shade and likes rich soil where it will seed itself, hybridizing freely with others, and apparently incapable of producing anything but beautiful offspring. Plant it under spring-flowering deciduous shrubs such as *Magnolia stellata*; it makes a marvellous background to crocuses and snowdrops.

Hesperis

Hesperis matronalis
Origin: S. Europe to
W. Asia
Height: 6ft/1.8m
Z: 6

There are about twenty-five species of hesperis, in the family Cruciferae, native to Asia and Europe.

❧ Sweet rocket possesses one of the half-dozen most delicious scents of any garden plant. It is at its most pronounced in the evening (hence the name) – heavy, rich, sweet and slightly peppery. It has tall stems and slightly toothed leaves, rounded and pointed. The flowers may be violet or, much better, white, and each flower is single, 1in/2.5cm across, with a lime-green eye. There are double-flowered forms, including a very

rare white, *H.m.* 'Alba Plena', which is gradually coming back into cultivation. It is an excellent border plant, looking wonderful with shrub roses with whose perfume it mingles to produce a stupendous cocktail of scents. It will flourish in semi-shade and seed itself (usually in the right place). Young plants flower best and older ones become woody and straggling.

Hosta 'Krossa Regal'

Hosta

There are forty species of hosta, in the family Liliaceae/Funkiaceae, all herbaceous perennials native to east Asia. The foliage is the great beauty of hostas, though some also have distinguished and long-lasting flowers. There has been an immense amount of hybridization in recent years, producing several hundreds of named cultivars. From the gardener's point of view there are only a few really outstanding varieties. Unless otherwise mentioned all need a shady position in moist humus-rich soil. They are beautiful in a woodland setting where old clumps of the larger-leaved kinds are among the few herbaceous plants that can hold their own, in terms of presence and decorative quality, with the woody plants surrounding them. All may be propagated by division; plants raised from the profusely carried seed will rarely breed true.

Hosta 'Krossa Regal'
Origin: Garden (Japan)
Height: 4ft/1.2m
Z: 3

❧ This is an exceptionally handsome example of the more recent cultivars. It has something of the character of *Hosta sieboldiana elegans* but its foliage is held on longer stems, giving it a more vertical emphasis. The leaves are up to 18in/45cm long, heart-shaped and pointed and of a striking glaucous-green. The flowers, purple-blue trumpets in June or July, are carried on tall stems high above the foliage. Of all the larger hostas this has perhaps the most emphatic structural quality; it looks magnificent as a regular punctuation mark in a grand (and shady) border.

Hosta plantaginea
Origin: China
Height: 24in/60cm
Z: 3

❧ This hosta has such elegance that it makes an excellent border plant. It is upright, with the very fresh green leaves held aloft, each up to 8in/20cm long, elegant heart-shapes with marked ribs. Its flowers, appearing very late in the summer or early autumn, are slender white trumpet-shapes up to 3in/8cm long and, uniquely among all hostas, with a delicious scent of positively tropical sweetness, most striking in the cool of the evening. I know of no other flower for temperate gardens of such sweet scent at that season of the year. There is a fine larger-flowered form, *H.p. grandiflora*, and a good hybrid (with *H. fortunei*) with the rather discouraging name of 'Honeybells' which has much of the character of the type, including its delicious scent, but foliage of a healthy lime-green.

Hosta sieboldiana elegans

Hosta sieboldiana
Origin: Japan
Height: 24in/60cm
Z: 3

❧ The foliage is all important here. In late spring sharp spikes of new growth emerge and by early June the dramatic leaves have reached their full size. They are widely heart-shaped, 12in/30cm across, curved and finely ribbed. In late June or July tall flower heads open, small, insignificant and an indeterminate faded blue-purple, an anti-climax to the splendour of the foliage. The form *H.s. elegans* is even more beautiful, with a very ornamental blueish cast to the leaves. *H.s.* 'Frances Williams' has handsome gold edges to the leaves. All these have powerful architectural shapes and may be used structurally in a border to great effect. It might be worth planning a shady damp one simply to accommodate these very distinguished plants. They may also be used in pots: a pair flanking a shady gateway is a handsome sight, but they will need moisture-retentive soil and plenty of watering.

Inula

There are about ninety species of inula, in the family Compositae, native to the temperate regions of Asia and Europe.

Inula magnifica
Origin: Caucasus
Height: 6ft/1.8m
Z: 6

❧ The name is right – this really is a magnificent plant. It has huge curving leaves with purple stems, up to 36in/90cm long at the base of the plant. Fleshy, hairy stems rise above this dramatic base, bearing smaller versions of the basal leaves (attractively mottled) and, in June, wonderfully decorative flower buds, intricate rosettes of green and purple. They open to brilliant dandelion-yellow flowers 5in/13cm across, composed of countless very narrow petals, making a flower that is simultaneously bold and delicate. It must have rich moist soil and will flower at its best in a sunny position. Its architectural presence can be used to give structure to the border.

Kirengeshoma

There are two species of kirengeshoma, in the family Hydrangeaceae, both native to Japan.

Kirengeshoma palmata
Origin: Japan
Height: 6ft/1.8m
Z: 5

❧ This beautiful plant performs rather differently from most herbaceous plants. The leaves appear in April, rounded, with pointed and toothed lobes, 6in/15cm across, a fresh light green emphatically marked with veins. The flowers, however, do not appear until very late in the season, in August or September, held high above the foliage on slender stems, trumpet-shaped, 2in/5cm long, a handsome pale yellow. It likes moist rich soil and is at its best in semi-shade. It has the reputation of demanding acid soil but I have seen it grown successfully in neutral soil. It may be propagated by division in late winter. Plant it in a shady mixed border near late-summer blue-flowered plants such as *Hydrangea aspera villosa*.

Knautia

There are sixty species of knautia, all herbaceous, in the family Dipsacaceae, native to Asia and Europe.

Knautia macedonica
Origin: Europe
Height: 24in/60cm
Z: 5

❧ The special charm of this plant is the combination of handsome grey foliage and an unusual deep purple-red flower. The leaves are narrow, pointed, deeply veined and 3in/8cm long, a silvery felted grey. The flowers, in May or June, are striking pincushions carried on slender hairy stems, 1½in/4cm across, deep purple but rather more red in brilliant sunshine. It prefers a dry well-drained place, will flourish in poor soil, and is at its darkest in semi-shade. It is an essential ingredient for red/purple colour schemes. It may be propagated by division or by seed.

Lamium

There are about forty species of lamium, in the family Labiatae, native to Asia and Europe.

Lamium orvala
Origin: S. Europe
Height: 12in/30cm
Z: 4

❧ This dead nettle has a rich and sombre combination of colours that is irresistible. The leaves unfurl in April, 2in/5cm long, rounded, pointed and toothed at the margin, a deep bluish-green; to be followed in May by

Lamium orvala

dusty purple-pink flowers with mottled lips, 1¹/₂in/4cm long. It makes a very good plant for a shady place in the border. It is easily propagated by division.

Lathyrus

Lathyrus latifolius
Origin: Europe
Height: 6ft/1.8m
Z: 5

There are over 100 species of lathyrus, or wild pea, all herbaceous plants, in the family Leguminosae, very widely distributed in North and South America, Africa, Asia and Europe.

🍃 The perennial ornamental pea, an old cottage garden plant, has many decorative virtues. The leaves, oval and pointed, up to 2¹/₂in/6cm long, are a fine glaucous-green with a paler tracery of veins. The curious strap-like stems sprawl, changing direction at odd angles, and are armed with fine curling tendrils which will cause the plant to climb upwards on any suitable surface. The flowers, carried in abundant trusses, opening from June for a very long period, are characteristic lipped pea flowers of a shocking but cheerful carmine-pink. It can be trained on a trellis or wall but its best use is in the mixed border where it may sprawl decoratively over other plants. I have seen it used to brilliant effect draped over the sombre form of the prostrate yew *Taxus baccata* 'Dovastoniana'. There is a beautiful white form, *L.l. albus*. Both like sun or semi-shade and may be propagated by seed, the latter producing a high proportion of white offspring.

Ligularia

Ligularia dentata
Origin: China, Japan
Height: 4ft/1.2cm
Z: 4

Ligularia przewalskii

Ligularia przewalskii
Origin: China
Height: 6ft/1.8m
Z: 4

There are about 180 species of ligularia, all herbaceous, in the family Compositae, all native to temperate regions of Asia and Europe.

❧ The leaves of this ligularia are heart-shaped and leathery, up to 12in/30cm across. The flowers, borne in June or July, are bright orange, daisy-like, 2in/5cm across. It needs moist soil in sun or semi-shade. It is easily propagated by division. A splendid and dramatic cultivar is *L.d.* 'Desdemona', whose leaves are khaki on the top and a sinister purple-brown underneath.

❧ The foliage of this ligularia is very decorative. It is round but very deeply cut with pointed lobes, 9in/23cm across. In June the flowers are carried on tall slender almost black stems. They are arranged in long spires, each flower diminutive, airy and elegant, a warm

rich yellow contrasting handsomely with the dark
stem. It must have a rich moist soil in full sun or
semi-shade. This is a plant that looks ridiculous planted
in any other way except as a bold clump. It may be
propagated by division or seed.

Linum

There are about 200 species of linum, in the family
Linaceae, widely distributed in the temperate
regions of the northern hemisphere.

Linum perenne
Origin: W. North America
Height: 24in/60cm
Z: 7

• This is the kind of small unobtrusive plant that has
presence and character out of proportion to its size.
The leaves are very narrow, pointed and glaucous-grey,
1in/2.5cm long. The flowers are produced on swaying
slender stems from June onwards – silvery blue saucers,
1–1¹/₂in/2.5–4cm across, veined with deeper blue and
splashed with lemon-yellow anthers at the centre. Each
flower is very short-lived, scattering blue petals on the
ground, but new buds seem constantly ready to replace
them. Taking up very little ground space in the border,
the flowered stems sway attractively over other lower
plants. It likes a sunny position and may be propagated
by seed or cuttings. *Linum narbonense* is very similar
in all respects except that it is a paler blue and has more
rounded petals.

Lobelia

There are at least 300 species of lobelia, both
herbaceous and woody, in the family
Campanulaceae, of which by far the greatest number
are native to Africa, America and Asia.

Lobelia tupa
Origin: Chile
Height: 6ft/1.8m
Z: 8

• Any gardener who possesses the right conditions to
allow this marvellous plant to flourish should acquire it
immediately. Its leaves, emerging fully in June, are very
distinguished: grey, felty, up to 12in/30cm long,
narrow, with wavy margins and pointed tips. The
flowers open in late July or August, among the most
dramatic you will ever see; they are borne on noble
spires, up to 18in/45cm long, each individual flower

tubular and hooked like the bill of an exotic bird. In colour the flower is a rich dusty red with a handsomely contrasting calyx coloured a browner red. The stamen protrudes markedly, with a curious silvery grey tip. It needs a very warm and sunny position, rich feeding and plenty of water. If you can provide this you will be rewarded by one of the most magnificent of all herbaceous plants, able to hold its own with anything else in the border. It may be propagated by division.

Lychnis

There are about twenty species of lychnis, in the family Caryophyllaceae, native to temperate areas of the northern hemisphere.

Lychnis chalcedonica
Origin: Russia
Height: 36in/90cm
Z: 4

In June this lychnis gives a splash of dazzling colour, a brilliant scarlet not quite like that of any other plant. It forms a bold clump of heart-shaped leaves, a good fresh green, from the midst of which stout stems bear corymbs of prolific diminutive flowers. Its place is in the border where the exciting colour of this simple plant will give an exotic note. It needs sun but not rich soil. It may be propagated by seed or division.

Lychnis coronaria
Origin: S.E. Europe
Height: 36in/90cm
Z: 6

The leaves of this lychnis are pale silver-grey and pointed, 1½in/4cm long and very decorative. The flowers, opening in June, are a startling rosy magenta with darker veins, single, 1½in/4cm across. It is, in leaf and flower, a very ornamental border plant, an excellent ingredient for a hot and lively scheme. It is best in a sunny position but flourishes in poor soil and although very short-lived, and at its best when young, is easy to propagate by seed or division. The flowers of a white form, *L.c.* 'Alba', are beautiful with the pale grey leaves.

Lychnis coronaria

Lysichiton

Lysichiton americanus
Origin: W. North America
Height: 4ft/1.2m
Z: 7

A genus of two moisture-loving plants in the family Araceae, native to Asia and North America.

❧ This bog arum is sometimes called skunk cabbage, which warns gardeners of its horrible smell – but everything else about it is attractive. It is a plant for the edges of streams or pools. In April curved lemon-yellow sails tinged with green make their appearance; these are the spathes which curve round to protect the cupped flower spike within. Late in the season come great bold shield-shaped leaves, of a fresh, glistening green. This is not a plant for delicate effects; it belongs in a wild and naturalistic setting where it has commanding presence. Apart from the essential requirement of moisture it has no special needs, growing equally well in sun or semi-shade. It is easy to propagate from seed. The Asian *L. camtschatcensis*, is virtually identical except that it has white spathes.

Lysichiton americanus

Lysimachia

Lysimachia clethroïdes
Origin: China, Japan
Height: 36in/90cm
Z: 4

Lysimachia ephemerum
Origin: S.W. Europe
Height: 5ft/1.5m
Z: 7

There are 150 species of lysimachia, or loosestrife, in the family Primulaceae, almost all herbaceous, and native to Africa, America and Asia.

❧ The twisting spires of soft white flowers in June make this a decorative ingredient in a romantic and exuberant border. The mid-green leaves are pointed, oval, up to 4in/10cm long, slightly speckled with black spots, and the flower stems are crowned with spires of star-shaped flowers up to 9in/23cm long. It is best in full sun and moist soil. It may be propagated by division.

❧ Grey and white are the essential colours of this stately loosestrife. It starts to make an impact in May or June when its beautiful soft grey foliage appears, each leaf up to 5in/13cm long, narrow and pointed. In late June or July the stems are crowned with spires of single grey-white flowers of ghostly distinction. This is an ideal border plant, adding subtly to richness of texture and fitting in with any colour scheme. It will flourish in part-shade and will do best in fertile moist soil. It may be propagated by division.

Malva

There are thirty species of malva, in the family Malvaceae, very widely distributed in Africa, Asia and Europe.

Malva moschata alba
Origin: Garden (Europe)
Height: 24in/60cm
Z: 3

≈ This is a form of the European native pink-mauve musk mallow, a common wildflower of waysides. The attractive leaves are very divided, up to 3in/8cm across, and rather hairy. The flowers are carried in profuse clusters at the tips of stems; dazzling, white, single, 1½in/3cm across, with the palest pink centre. Unless supported it will sprawl attractively and is a lovely border plant, straggling through others. It will thrive in sun or semi-shade where its white flowers are seen to best effect. It may be propagated by division.

Matteuccia

There are about four species of matteuccia, in the family Dryopteridaceae, native to North America, Asia and Europe.

Matteuccia struthiopteris
Origin: North America, Asia, Europe
Height: 4ft/1.2m
Z: 2

❧ The shuttlecock fern is at once dramatic and refined. It produces its beautiful upright fronds in late spring, pale green and curving elegantly outwards towards the top. They are pinnate, each delicately toothed leaflet up to 4in/10cm long. This is a plant that needs at least part shade; it looks yellow and sickly in full sun. It is said also to demand moisture but I grow it successfully in a dry site at the foot of a north-facing wall. It has rather invasive roots and is at its most beautiful in a woodland setting where its crisp architectural beauty is striking throughout the season. It may be propagated by removing and potting up the side 'crowns' at the foot of the plant.

Meconopsis

There are about fifty species of meconopsis, in the family Papaveraceae, native to east Asia and Europe.

Meconopsis betonicifolia
(*M. baileyi*)
Origin: China
Height: 4ft/1.2m
Z: 7

❧ This great Himalayan poppy is not easy to please but in the right garden will give intense pleasure. From the centre of rosettes of rather hairy leaves, pale silver when young, slender stems arise in May or June carrying single flowers, 2in/5cm across, a dazzling sky

Illustration opposite:
Melianthus major

Meconopsis cambrica

Meconopsis cambrica
Origin: Europe
Height: 10in/25cm
Z: 6

blue with hints of silver. To perform properly it needs a cool moist acid soil of the sort that suits rhododendrons. As a woodland plant it has unique distinction.

❧ The Welsh poppy is an invasive plant, seeding with vigour, but it is very ornamental. It forms burgeoning mounds of fresh pale green pinnate foliage with slightly toothed and pointed lobes. The flowers come out in April, varying in colour from very pale lemon to a rich orange, of papery texture, $1^{1}/_{2}$in/4cm across, carried on very slender wiry stems. There are sterile double forms which are also very decorative and have the advantage of not seeding themselves. They do very well in almost any soil and flourish in the shade where they look marvellous among mossy rocks, ferns and lily-of-the-valley. I grow it with pale blue irises; the colours set each other off admirably.

Melianthus

Melianthus major
Origin: South Africa
Height: 8ft/2.5m
Z: 9

There are six species of melianthus, in the family Melianthaceae, native to southern Africa.

❧ The exquisite foliage of this plant puts it into the very first division of ornamental plants. The leaves are curving pinnate fronds, each leaflet toothed, rounded and up to 3in/8cm long and in colour a cool glaucous-green. In moist fertile soil in a sunny position

it will put on at least 4ft/1.2m of growth in a season; in very mild gardens it will not be cut back in winter and you may see the flowers in the following spring, which are borne on old growth. They are curious rather than beautiful, a froth of brown plumes exuding the honey nectar which gives the plant its name. It may be propagated by division.

Nepeta

There are about 250 species of nepeta, all herbaceous, in the family Labiatae, native to Africa, Asia and Europe.

Nepeta × faassenii
Origin: Garden
Height: 24in/60cm
Z: 3

❧ Catmint is an essential cottage garden plant that has its decorative uses in any garden. The leaves are a handsome grey-green, 1in/2.5cm long, toothed and redolent of that aromatic scent that cats love. From June onwards, spikes of flowers, pale lavender, look beautiful against the mounds of foliage. A sunny position is best and if it is cut back after the first great flush of flowers, there will be a second display. In many old gardens it is used to line paths where its lax stems blur hard edges. In the mixed border it is wonderful under shrub roses, especially those with pink or purple flowers. It may be propagated by division.

Nepeta 'Souvenir d'André Chaudron'
Origin: Garden
Height: 24in/60cm
Z: 5

❧ This nepeta is of uncertain origin but undoubted charm. It forms upright stems, with aromatic toothed leaves up to 3in/8cm long; the tips of the stems are crowned in late June or July with dusty violet buds which open to reveal pure blue single flowers, tubular and lipped, 1in/2.5cm long. In the border it straggles through other plants and is excellent with creams or pale yellows. It flowers best in sun or semi-shade. It has spreading roots but not uncontrollably so and may be very easily propagated by division.

Oenothera

There are about 120 species of oenothera, all herbaceous, in the family Onagraceae, and native to the Americas.

Oenothera missouriensis
Origin: S. North America
Height: 4in/10cm
Z: 5

❧ This low-growing evening primrose has wonderfully beautiful flowers. The leaves are dark green, narrow and pointed, up to 3in/8cm long; the plant hugs the ground and the leaves form a loose spreading mat. The flowers, starting in June and continuing for weeks, are single, pale yellow, of a glowing intensity with deeper gold towards the centre. They open in the evening, lovely saucers up to 4in/10cm across, and when they close the petals lie gracefully folded. In the border it looks wonderful at the feet of pale blue campanulas. It must have a sunny position and will not tolerate waterlogged heavy soil. It may be propagated by seed.

Omphalodes

There are about twenty species of this genus, in the family Boraginaceae, all herbaceous plants. Their natural habitat ranges from east Asia to the Mediterranean countries.

Omphalodes cappadocica
Origin: Asia, Caucasus
Height: 5in/12.5cm
Z: 6

❧ The brilliant blue of this little navelwort is not easily found in any other spring-flowering plant. Purple-pink buds open in April to reveal single flowers ¹/₂in/1.25cm across, of a clear but intense blue, with a white eye and pink veins. The leaf, a slender heart-shape, is a fresh green. It is a wonderful plant to grow in a wall or at the edge of a dry sunny border. I grow it alongside the feathery foliage of *Dicentra formosa* whose soft, pinkish-red flowers go admirably with it. It is very easily propagated by division.

Paeonia

Illustration opposite:
Paeonia mlokosewitschii

There are over thirty species of peony, mostly herbaceous but a few shrubs, in the family Paeoniaceae, widely distributed in North America, Asia and Europe. They have a short flowering period but many have very beautiful foliage which continues the interest. There are well over 100 named cultivars, mostly of *Paeonia lactiflora*, some of which have very large double flowers, decorative in themselves but making the plant top-heavy. Here I have picked out

one or two species which I consider particularly garden worthy. All like a sunny position in rich but well-drained soil. Peonies may be propagated by root division in autumn or, for species, by freshly sown seed.

Paeonia mlokosewitschii
Origin: Caucasus
Height: 24in/60cm
Z: 5

❧ With only a brief – but glorious – flowering period, this lovely peony has exceptionally fine foliage, rounded and glaucous-grey. The single flowers open in April or May from plump buds, at first resembling huge buttercups but spreading into a cupped shape, 4in/10cm across, a very pale yellow with the faintest flush of peach; the crowded egg-yolk yellow stamens give off the true peony scent, a curious mixture of warm rubber and peppercorns. The leaves are oval and pointed, 4in/10cm long, of a very handsome grey-green, and the whole plant forms a well-rounded bushy shape, harmonious in all its parts. It is the ideal border plant, preserving its distinguished identity but consorting easily with other plants.

Paeonia officinalis

Paeonia officinalis
Origin: S. Europe
Height: 24in/60cm
Z: 3

❧ The commonest garden peony is a striking border plant. Its handsome foliage unfolds in April, generous hand-shaped leaves of which each leaflet is 4in/10cm long and decoratively veined. The plump flower buds open in May, blood-red, single or very double and with the distinctive peony scent (see above). The leaves continue to give pleasure long after the flowers have fallen. It does best in moist fertile soil and a sunny position and may be propagated by dividing the fleshy roots in the autumn.

Paeonia tenuifolia
Origin: Caucasus
Height: 18in/45cm
Z: 4

❧ The foliage is the distinctive thing about this peony. It is very finely divided, forming palm-like fronds spreading delicately outwards. The flowers rise above in May, single and a dazzling crimson set off by rich yellow stamens. Being fairly low, it is an excellent plant near the edge of a border. Smaller herbaceous plants like potentillas and pinks happily grow through its beautiful leaves which will give ornament throughout the growing season.

Penstemon

Penstemon 'Hidcote Pink'

There are about 250 species of penstemon, in the family Scrophulariaceae, almost all of which are native to western North America. Those grown in gardens are usually cultivars of frequently unknown hybrids. All need a sunny protected position in well-drained soil, are evergreen or semi-evergreen and may be propagated by cuttings. Naming is extremely difficult as the same plant is known under different names. All have tubular flowers with a flared opening, borne over a very long flowering period, starting in June, which makes them valuable border plants. In a mixed border they will stray among other plants, giving an attractive atmosphere of abundance. In colour they range from white, blue, pink, red to various shades of purple. The best, to my taste, are the pinks, reds and purples; some have contrasting colours.

'Garnet' grows to 36in/90cm, forming a vigorous bush with wine-red flowers. 'Hidcote Pink' is 30in/75cm high with especially decorative old-fashioned muddy pink flowers. 'Port Wine' is 24in/60cm high with deep dusty purple flowers and a wide, pale throat rather larger than most: these are up to 1¹/₂in/4cm long; 'Torquay Gem' is 24in/60cm high, with slender blood-red flowers and white throats laced with red. All these are hardy to Zone 4.

Phygelius

Phygelius capensis
Origin: South Africa
Height: 5ft/1.5m
Z: 8

Illustration above:
Phygelius aequalis
'Yellow Trumpet'

There are two species of phygelius, in the family Scrophulariaceae, native to South Africa.

❧ Although this is a shrub up to 10ft/3m in its native habitat, in cooler climates it will be cut back in winter most years, and is better thought of as a herbaceous perennial. It throws out fleshy growth with dark brown stems and toothed heart-shaped leaves 1½in/4cm long. The flowers, starting in June but continuing throughout the growing season, are bunches of hanging tubes with a scalloped outward-curving mouth, 2in/5cm long, a rich orange-scarlet. It must have a sunny protected position and it may be trained against a wall, which in warmer gardens could provide enough protection for it to pass the winter unscathed. In the border it is a beautiful plant for hot colour schemes. It may be propagated by cuttings or division. *P. aequalis* is similar in all respects but the flowers are an especially beautiful shade of dusty pink. There is a cultivar, *P.a.* 'Yellow Trumpet', that has very handsome flowers of pale creamy yellow.

Polemonium

There are about twenty-five species of polemonium, all herbaceous, in the family Polemoniaceae, native to the cooler parts of the northern hemisphere and South America.

Polemonium caeruleum album

Polemonium caeruleum
Origin: North America,
N. Asia, N. Europe
Height: 36in/90cm
Z: 2

❧ It is hard to believe that this exuberant plant is native to the Arctic regions. The leaves appear in April, feathery pinnate foliage 4in/10cm long, each diminutive leaflet creased down its axis. The flowers in June are carried abundantly in crowded bunches at the tips of stems ³/₄in/1.5cm across, with yellow anthers and dark veining within. There is a very pretty white form, *P.c. album*. Both are marvellous border plants, with distinguished and lively foliage and generous blossom. It likes heavy damp soil in sun or semi-shade. It seeds itself rather liberally but not uncontrollably.

143

Polystichum

There are over 175 species of polystichum ferns, in the family Dryopteridaceae, distributed in every continent.

Polystichum setiferum
Origin: Europe
Height: 36in/90cm
Z: 7

❧ There has been a lively renewal of interest in ferns and they do make beautiful and trouble-free garden plants. The soft shield fern is evergreen or semi-evergreen and has sideways-curving fronds, intricately pinnate, up to 18in/45cm long. The new foliage appears in spring, upright and curled, resembling the neck of a fiddle, with russet central veins and silver downy new foliage – a dazzling sight. There is an immense number of cultivars, some with densely packed overlapping foliage, and none without charm; but the type itself is a splendidly ornamental plant. It is a plant for shade; I grow it in very dry conditions where it seems entirely at ease. It may be propagated by division or seed.

Potentilla

There are about 500 species of potentilla, herbaceous and woody, in the family Rosaceae, very widely distributed in the northern hemisphere. For the woody kinds see pages 211–12.

Potentilla atrosanguinea
Origin: Himalaya
Height: 18in/45cm
Z: 5

❧ This is a very beautiful and wonderfully versatile plant. The leaves are a fresh green, three-part, rounded, veined and toothed, up to 4in/10cm across. The flowers, from June onwards, are produced at the tips of trailing stems and are of a marvellous deep scarlet, slightly cupped, 1in/2.5cm across and with a pale yellow centre. It is excellent for a sunny position to the front of the border where it will mingle with other plants. I grow it wandering through pinks and the deep purple leaves of *Salvia officinalis* 'Purpurascens'. *P.a. argyrophylla* has much paler leaves rimmed with silver and with silver undersides, an exquisite contrast to the flowers. It is very easily propagated by division, which should be done every three or four years to maintain vigorous plants.

Potentilla atrosanguinea

Potentilla nepalensis
Origin: Himalaya
Height: 24in/60cm
Z: 5

❧ This has much in common with the above but the leaves are much narrower. The flowers, borne profusely on the tips of red-flushed stems from June onwards for a long season, are 1¹/₂in/4cm across and have rounded petals, a purplish red with a darker eye. 'Miss Willmott' is an excellent warm pink. They should be planted in a sunny position and may be propagated by division.

Primula

Primula Candelabra
hybrids
Origin: Garden
Height: 24–36in/
60–90cm
Z: 5

There are well over 500 species of primula in the family Primulaceae, most of which are natives of the temperate regions of the northern hemisphere. A large number of them are alpines, often very beautiful but requiring cultivation that few gardeners are able easily to provide. I have chosen here a few trouble-free kinds that are especially garden worthy.

❧ The Candelabra group of primulas are hybrids and cultivars of Asiatic species. They flower in early summer and show great variation in colour – white, pink, orange, crimson and purple. They have in common flowers that are either arranged in whorls up the stem (such as the splendid wine-coloured *P. pulverulenta*) or in the form of a rounded 'drumstick' such as *P. japonica*. They must have a cool moist site in part shade. They are wonderful in bold drifts in informal woodland, but beware some of the more strident colours which can give a false note. They may be propagated by division.

Primula japonica
'Stopford White'

Primula florindae
Origin: Tibet
Height: 24in/60cm
Z: 6

❧ This lovely primula is a superb ornament for edging the banks of a stream or pool. From mats of bold shield-shaped foliage, tall flower stems carry hanging bunches of sweetly scented pale yellow flowers in June, lasting for weeks. This is a plant for the wild garden where it will easily establish a colony in moist soil and part shade. It may be propagated by seed or, for cultivars, by division.

Primula vulgaris alba
'Flore Pleno'

Primula vulgaris
Origin: W. and S. Europe
Height: 6in/15cm
Z: 6

❧ The wild European primrose is an irresistibly beautiful hedgerow plant, and in the garden an essential spring flower. The leaves appear in February or March, 4–6in/10–15cm long, oval, leathery and heavily veined. The flowers emerge shortly afterwards, characteristically a pale creamy yellow, $1^1/_2$in/4cm across, single, with a deeper golden eye and suffused with a delicate pure sweet scent. It is at its best in moist heavy soil in shade or semi-shade where it will self-seed freely. In the wild the colour varies from white to pink and there are several shades of yellow. An especially attractive variety is the double-flowered white *P.v. alba* 'Flore Pleno'. These are not plants for the formal border; they are at their best planted generously in an orchard or woodland.

Pulmonaria

A genus of seven species, in the family Boraginaceae, native to Europe, the Near East and northern Asia. They are easy to propagate by dividing the plants in the autumn.

Pulmonaria longifolia
Origin: N. Europe
Height: 6in/15cm
Z: 5

❧ The foliage is the thing with this pulmonaria. The leaves are long, slender and pointed and they overlap to form a most elegant mound. Clear vivid blue flowers at the end of long stems appear in April or May. In the wild it is found in semi-shade, and given a similar site in the garden it will do well and the blue flowers will not be bleached by the sun.

Pulmonaria officinalis
Origin: Europe
Height: 8in/20cm
Z: 4

❧ Spotted Dog or Soldiers and Sailors, to take two of its many common names, is in its wild form a cheerful but rather coarse plant. However, there is a white cultivar, *P.o.* 'Sissinghurst White', which is splendidly ornamental. The pure white hanging bell-shaped flowers appear in March on long stems rising above the characteristic downy mid-green foliage, splashed with spots of paler green. It prefers partial shade and will perform admirably in a dry shaded position where its subtle colours are at their best.

Pulmonaria officinalis
'Sissinghurst White'

Pulmonaria saccharata
Origin: Europe
Height: 10in/30cm
Z: 4

This lungwort has outstandingly fine leaves – up to 4in/10cm long, elegantly pointed, and pale green handsomely spotted with an irregular marbling of paler spots. The flowers, emerging in April from very deep purple buds, are a fresh rosy pink which turns blue as they age. It is a woodland plant and looks wonderful with cyclamen, ferns and hellebores. There is a good white-flowered form, *P.s.* 'Alba', and a marvellous one with silver frosting to the foliage, *P.s.* 'Argentea'.

Pulsatilla

There are about thirty species of pulsatilla, in the family Ranunculaceae, native to North America, Asia and Europe.

Pulsatilla vulgaris
Origin: Europe
Height: 6in/15cm
Z: 5

The Pasque flower, usually flowering well before Easter, is found in the wild on open high limestone or chalk. The flowers are borne on erect stems and are 2in/5cm long, bell-shaped, opening out with pointed petals, blue-purple in colour with abundant egg-yolk

Illustration opposite:
Pulsatilla vulgaris

yellow stamens within. The outer petals, stems and foliage are brushed with silvery down. The foliage, grey and very deeply and finely cut, is of the utmost elegance. In its detail and as a whole it is an irresistibly beautiful plant that must be given a sunny, very well-drained position, and is, alas, not easy to site in the garden. I have seen it looking marvellous alongside the sombre purple foliage of the sage *Salvia officinalis* 'Purpurascens' which relishes the same conditions. It is best propagated by seed.

Romneya

There is only one species of the genus romneya in the family Papaveraceae.

Romneya coulteri
Origin: California, Mexico
Height: 5ft/1.5m
Z: 7

❧ The Californian tree poppy has strikingly beautiful foliage – glaucous grey-green, each leaf most elegantly cut, up to 4in/10cm long. The flowers open in late June or July from plump bristly buds; they are single, white, up to 6in/15cm, with overlapping papery petals and a mound of egg-yolk yellow stamens; they have a curious smell like old-fashioned washing powder. It needs a sunny position and is admirable in the border where its beautiful foliage is decorative throughout the growing season. Many gardeners complain either that it is very difficult to establish or that, once established, it is intolerably invasive. The recommended method of propagation is by root cuttings, which are difficult.

Salvia

The sages constitute an immense genus with over 500 species, woody and herbaceous, in the family Labiatae, very widely distributed. For woody varieties see pages 221–22.

Salvia uliginosa
Origin: South America
Height: 8ft/2.4m
Z: 8

❧ There is no plant remotely comparable to this and any gardener with the conditions that suit it should certainly have it. It starts to grow in late spring, throwing out tall swaying stems bearing toothed aromatic leaves 2in/5cm long. Brilliant sky-blue flowers like miniature snapdragons appear at the tips of the stems in August and continue until the first frosts. This is a marvellous plant for a sunny position in the border, for it takes up little ground space and soars above other plants, its flowers waving gracefully. Its specific name means 'of swamps', yet although it relishes fertile soil, too much moisture will kill it in a cold winter. It is easy to propagate, both by seed (which it obligingly does for you) and by division in early spring. It should in any case be divided every three or four years as it tends to form a woody base that inhibits flowering growth.

Scabiosa

There are about sixty species of scabiosa, in the family Dipsacaceae, native to Africa, Asia and Europe.

Scabiosa caucasica
Origin: Caucasus
Height: 18in/45cm
Z: 4

❧ For a long-lasting display of attractive flowers there are few herbaceous perennials to beat this scabious. From mounds of deeply cut grey-green foliage slender stems bear flowers from June onwards through the growing season. Each flower is 2in/5cm across, a plump pincushion of pale blue, often too heavy for the stem to hold aloft without support. It is best in a sunny position in well-drained soil and it may be propagated by seed or by division. Young plants flower best so it is advisable to propagate every three or four years. There are several cultivars: 'Clive Greaves' has much larger (up to 3in/8cm across) flowers with attractively frilly edges, a delicate lavender-blue with a contrasting paler centre; 'Moerheim Blue' is a powerful blue; and 'Miss Willmott' an excellent creamy white.

Sidalcea

There are twenty species of sidalcea, all herbaceous, in the family Malvaceae, all native to western North America.

Sidalcea candida
Origin: W. North America
Height: 36in/90cm
Z: 5

❧ The leaves of this mallow are boldly palm-shaped, 5in/12cm across, and form a mound. The flowers are carried in delicate spires from June onwards; they are single, 1 1/2in/3cm across, a ghostly grey-white with pale purple centres. In a sunny position, in rich soil, it will carry flowers over a very long period and is an admirable plant for the front of the border. It may be propagated by division. There are some beautiful cultivars of uncertain parentage, with flowers of very decorative colours: 'Croftway Red' is a vibrant blood-red; 'Sussex Beauty' is a marvellous pink.

Stipa

Stipa tenuissima
Origin: S. North America and Central America
Height: 36in/90cm
Z: 7

A genus of about 300 species of grasses, in the family Gramineae, widely distributed in the warm temperate regions.

❧ This perennial grass has lime-green stems which produce the most spectacular and beautiful seed heads in June: pale gold flecked with purple, the texture of the finest spun silk; the crowded panicles up to 12in/30cm long sway in the breeze like the mane of some exotic and distinguished horse. To emphasize this effect it should be planted in bold clumps where it will mix easily with other plantings, except those that are clumsy and less aristocratic – defects will be mercilessly

exposed by the juxtaposition. It needs a sunny position in light well-drained soil and may be propagated by seed or division.

Stylophorum

A genus of three species, in the family Papaveraceae, native to North America and China.

Stylophorum diphyllum
Origin: E. North America
Height: 12in/30cm
Z: 5

☙ This is a woodland plant in its native habitat, flourishing in moist humus-rich soil. It has very fine leaves, hairy, mid-green and deeply lobed rather like an oak leaf. The nodding poppy-like flowers are suspended aloft from April onwards, a rich burnished yellow, 1 1/2in/4cm across. The seed pods in late summer are an attractive silver. In a shady place in the garden it looks wonderful with other shade-loving plants of distinctive foliage, such as Solomon's seal, ferns and hellebores. It may be propagated by division in autumn.

Symphytum

There are about thirty-five species of symphytum, all herbaceous, in the family Boraginaceae, widely distributed in the Caucasus, Europe and Asia.

Symphytum x *uplandicum*
'Variegatum'
Origin: Garden
Height: 36in/90cm
Z: 5

☙ Variegated plants are often difficult to place in a garden, introducing a strident or a bilious note. In this variegated comfrey the combination of leaf and flower colour is harmonious and satisfying. The leaves are oval and pointed, up to 4in/10cm long, and deeply veined.

They emerge fully in late April and are of a beautiful grey-green, occasionally mottled with a paler colour and with irregular margins of soft cream. In late May and June the flowers appear, small pendulous tubes, not spectacular but of a subtle blue that goes beautifully with the foliage. It will thrive in a position of semi-shade and will reward rich feeding. After flowering it has a tendency to become straggly and if cut back will produce a second flush of young foliage.

Symphytum × uplandicum 'Variegatum'

Thalictrum

Thalictrum aquilegiifolium
Origin: Asia, Europe
Height: 5ft/1.5m
Z: 6

There are about 130 species of thalictrum, all herbaceous, in the family of Ranunculaceae, very widely distributed in temperate and tropical regions.

❧ In the wild this stately plant grows in moist places in woods or grassland. Its leaves, rounded and lobed, 1¹/₂in/3cm across, are a fine glaucous grey-green. The flowers, carried on tall stems in May or June, are frothy mop-heads up to 6in/16cm across, varying in colour from white to pinky mauve or purple. It is a beautiful border plant, especially for fertile soil, and tolerates shade well. Its light feathery flowers rise decoratively above other plantings. There are several cultivars, of which *T.a.* 'Purpureum', a lovely deep purple, is marvellous in a scheme involving reds and purples. It may be propagated by seed or division.

Thalictrum delavayi
Origin: China
Height: 4ft/1.2m
Z: 7

❧ This Chinese thalictrum is very similar to the above but slightly smaller, with more open heads of flowers and with smaller, beautifully refined foliage. There is a striking form, *T.d.* 'Magnificum', with especially large flowers.

Trollius

There are about twenty species of trollius, in the family Ranunculaceae, with widely distributed habitats in North America, Asia and Europe.

Trollius europaeus
'Superbus'
Origin: Garden
Height: 24in/60cm
Z: 4

❧ A selection of the European globe flower, this is a border plant of cool distinction. The leaves, appearing in April, are deeply divided, like miniature vine leaves, 4in/10cm across. Above them the flowers are held aloft in May, irregular spheres, a glowing lemon-yellow 1½in/4cm across. Only the outer petals open slightly, so that the flowers preserve their globular shape until they fall. It likes heavy moist soil in sun or semi-shade and may be propagated by division in late autumn.

Veronica

A genus of about 250 species in the family Scrophulariaceae, widely distributed in both hemispheres.

Veronica gentianoïdes
Origin: Caucasus
Height: 12in/30cm
Z: 4

❧ This evergreen plant forms rosettes of shining rich green foliage, 4in/10cm across, from the centre of which splendid spires of the palest blue flowers rear up in late April or May. They are short-lived but wonderful, of ghostly delicacy. It likes a position in sun or semi-shade and will spread gently to form glistening mats of foliage, very decorative at the edge of a border. It is very easily propagated by division in autumn.

Veronicastrum

There are two species of veronicastrum, both herbaceous, in the family Scrophulariaceae, native to North America and north-east Asia.

Veronicastrum virginicum
Origin: N.E. North America
Height: 6ft/1.8m
Z: 3

❧ This beautiful North American native plant should be more widely seen in gardens. Narrow toothed leaves in ruffs along tall stems culminate in July in dramatic slender spires of flowers, either purple-blue or white in colour. The white is very much to be preferred and, massed at the back of a substantial border, forms an emphatic but ethereal airy curtain with a pronounced vertical emphasis. In the wild it is a plant of damp places and deep moist soil will suit it well in the garden. It may be propagated by division.

Veronicastrum virginicum album

Viola

There are about 500 species of violas, in the family Violaceae, native to northern temperate areas. Many are beautiful but few are big enough to make really valuable garden plants. It is easy to establish colonies of them but they hybridize very freely and their identity may soon be lost.

Viola cornuta
Origin: Spain
Height: 12in/30cm
Z: 7

❧ This is one of those valuable plants whose true worth is seen in association with other plantings. The flowers, a rich blue-violet, appear in May, single, 1¹/₂in/4cm across, with the backward-pointing 'horns' that gives the plant its name. It will scramble through other plants, producing flowers throughout the growing season. In late summer it may be cut back, which will stimulate new growth and flowers. There is a very pretty white form, *V.c. alba*, and a form much darker than the type, *V.c. purpurea*. It performs best in moist fertile soil and may be propagated by division or by cuttings.

Viola labradorica
'Purpurea'
Origin: Garden
Height: 3in/8cm
Z: 2

❧ The purple-leaved Labrador violet has decorative heart-shaped leaves up to 2in/5cm across, strikingly coloured with a purple cast. The flowers in April or May are blue-violet, looking very handsome against the foliage. This is an almost intolerably invasive plant, but in some wilder part of the garden, notably in dry shade, it will provide ornamental ground-cover. Do not, above all, let it loose in your choicest borders (I did!).

SHRUBS

Shrubs form the indispensable plant structure of a garden. By shrubs I mean all those woody plants that are neither trees nor need the support or protection of a wall. In the mixed border, which has become the most widely used kind of garden bed, a skilful planting of herbaceous plants may well provide dramatic structure for part of the year, but it is the solid, long-lasting presence of shrubs that gives the border, and hence the garden, its character. Here, too, repeat plantings of a distinctive shrub can provide unity and harmony to the composition of the whole.

The foliage colour of shrubs is immensely varied. As well as the many plants that have excellent evergreen foliage to give colour in winter, there are others that have beautiful leaves of grey or silver, dramatic purple, every shade of green from the palest lime-green to glistening dark green, and subtle variegations of cream and gold. These qualities of foliage, or distinction of shape or habit, are especially important in smaller gardens where space cannot be squandered on shrubs whose only virtue is a brief period of flowering, however magnificent. There is always a shrub of the right size and shape to meet the needs of any garden circumstance, and some may be clipped to give precisely the kind of architectural emphasis that is required.

The special value of shrubs in the garden is emphasized by the fact that I have yet to mention their flowering qualities. But there is no month in the year which is not ornamented by one shrub or another in flower, and these flowers are wide-ranging in colour and form, frequently

161

deliciously scented, and often prolific. It is easy to nominate shrubs the stars of the garden. But unlike many stars they do not always clamour for attention and attempt to overpower other players on the stage.

Abelia

Abelia × grandiflora
Origin: Garden
Height: 6ft/1.8m
Z: 7

There are about fifteen species of abelia, all woody, in the family Caprifoliaceae, all native to Central America and east Asia.

❧ This evergreen shrub never ceases to be decorative. The leaves, carried on dark red new growth, are 1in/2.5cm long, curvaceous and pointed, glistening and flushed with bronze. The flowers in July are small pink bells, with a slight sweet fragrance, borne in tremendous profusion. Long after they have fallen, the remaining soft pink sepals, looking curiously like a second flush of a quite different flower, remain to decorate the bush deep into winter. It flowers on the current season's growth and may be pruned in spring to

form a shapely rounded bush which will make a
beautiful ornament and an excellent vehicle for late-
flowering clematis; I allow the exotic large-flowered
rich red 'Gravetye Beauty' to stray decoratively
through it. It will flower well only if it has a sunny
protected position. It may be propagated by cuttings.

Abelia schumanii
Origin: China
Height: 4ft/1.2m
Z: 7

❧ This deciduous Chinese abelia is similar to the
above but it makes a more compact bush and the
flowers have a warm mauve flush that is very striking.
A. 'Edward Goucher' is a hybrid between this and
A. × grandiflora; it has the rosy flowers of the one, but
produced more freely, and the handsome evergreen
foliage of the other. It is a beautiful shrub for the
smaller garden.

Abutilon

There are about 100 species of abutilon in the family
Malvaceae, native to tropical and sub-tropical
regions.

Abutilon vitifolium
Origin: Chile
Height: 12ft/3.6m
Z: 8

❧ This evergreen shrub has pale green vine-like leaves,
very much paler on the underside, up to 4in/10cm long,
carried on attractively felty stems. The flowers in May
or June are single, a very striking silvery lilac,
2^{1}/2in/6cm across, carried in profuse bunches at the end
of stems. It has no special soil requirements but must

be in a sunny position. It is a marvellous plant for the back of a border, where its flowering branches and decorative foliage may soar above other plantings. The shrub is shallow-rooted; this, and a tendency to grow leggy, makes it vulnerable to wind. It should be pruned back after flowering which will both make a better-shaped plant and promote flowering the following year. It is in any case not long-lived and cuttings are easily taken in summer. It will also seed itself in an uninvasive sort of way. There is an excellent white form, *A.v. album.*

Aesculus

There are thirteen species of aesculus, in the family Hippocastanaceae, native to North America, Asia, Europe and India.

Aesculus parviflora
Origin: North America
Height: 12ft/3.6m
Z: 5

❧ Space is needed to get the spectacular best from this deciduous shrub for it suckers very freely, forming a broad thicket. The leaves, unfolding in April, are very beautiful. At first they hang downwards, like cloth draped over a framework, a marvellous pink-brown colour and strikingly veined. When mature they become bright green and the hand-shaped leaves are 12in/30cm across, but continue to droop rather elegantly. The flowers, in August, are a very valuable late summer ornament, spires of feathery white up to 12in/30cm long, borne handsomely above the leaves. In character it is very much a plant for a wild informal setting. It does well in semi-shade, and bulbs in March and April make an excellent ornament to the bare stems. It is propagated by digging up a rooted sucker.

Aralia

Aralia elata
Origin: China, Japan, Korea
Height: 15ft/4.5m
Z: 4

There are about forty species of aralia, in the family Araliaceae, native to American and Asia.

❧ The Japanese angelica tree makes a characterful spreading shrub, the very epitome of Eastern exoticism. It is deciduous, with immense doubly pinnate fronds of foliage whose leaflets are up to 6in/15cm long, curved and pointed. They are borne on spreading fleshy stems, pink in their youth. In late summer billowing upright panicles of creamy white flowers are borne, up to 24in/60cm long. It likes rich moist soil and will thrive in semi-shade or sun. It may be propagated by seed or suckers. *A.e.* 'Variegata' has beautiful, rather grey foliage splashed with cream at the margins;

Aralia elata 'Variegata'

A.e. 'Aureovariegata' is a golden-variegated counterpart. Less vigorous than the type they make striking plants for the border. They may be propagated only by grafting, a tricky job best left to professionals.

Arbutus

There are about twenty species of arbutus, in the family Ericaceae, widely distributed in North America, Asia Minor and Europe.

Arbutus unedo
Origin: Asia Minor, Europe
Height: 30ft/10m
Z: 8

❧ Everything is beautiful about this evergreen shrub or tree. Its foliage, narrowly oval and slightly toothed, is a sparkling rich green, contrasting finely with the pinkish new growth of the branches. At the end of the summer drooping bunches of little wax-textured urn-shaped cream flowers appear, remaining to the winter and hanging simultaneously with the spherical rough-textured fruit, 3/4in/2cm in diameter, which ripens to a dazzling vermilion. It does best in rich non-alkaline soil, in sun or semi-shade, and may be propagated from seed or cuttings. With age it forms a distinguished sprawling shape of tremendous character and, by removing lower branches, you can encourage it to form a tree shape with spreading canopy. A hybrid,

A. × *andrachnoïdes*, is similar but slightly smaller and has the additional attraction of beautiful peeling reddish-brown bark on old wood.

Artemisia

There are over 400 species, woody and herbaceous, in this genus, in the family Compositae, whose natural habitat is in the northern hemisphere and South America. For herbaceous species see page 79.

Artemisia arborescens
Origin: E. Mediterranean
Height: 24–36in/
60–90cm
Z: 8

❧ As a background to other low-growing plants there are few small shrubs that possess such beautiful foliage as this artemisia. It is of the palest silvery grey, very finely cut to form feathery fronds which have an agreeably pungent scent, like old varnish. The dirty yellow flowers in very late summer are a disappointment, but since the foliage is so beautiful, can be overlooked. The best form of all, *A.a.* 'Faith Raven', collected high in the mountains of Corfu and therefore less tender, has even more finely dissected leaves than the type. Repeat plantings of this short-lived shrub (which is very easy to propagate from cuttings) give harmony to a sunny border. It must have an open well-drained site and it will do well in poor stony soil. It has naturally a rather sprawling habit and may be encouraged into a more densely bushy shape by clipping firmly in March or April.

Buddleja

Buddleja alternifolia
Origin: China
Height: 10ft/3m
Z: 6

Buddleja colvilei
Origin: Himalaya
Height: 10ft/3m
Z: 8

Buddleja crispa
Origin: N. India
Height: 8ft/2.5m
Z: 8

Illustration opposite:
Buddleja crispa

There are at least 100 species of buddleja, in the family Loganiaceae, widely distributed in the warmer regions of both hemispheres.

This has a naturally weeping growth and may be encouraged to form a spectacular cascade of sweetly scented flowers. It is deciduous and flowers on the previous year's growth, which therefore needs hard pruning after flowering. It is possible to train an upright trunk, from the top of which the slender branches with their narrow pointed mid-green leaves will gracefully fall. The flowers in May, profuse bunches of diminutive lilac-blue, appear all along the branches, very sweetly scented. An attractive cultivar is the grey-leaved *B.a.* 'Argentea'. It does best in a sunny position but has no special soil requirements and may be propagated by cuttings.

This is a a stately aristocrat among the buddlejas, with dazzling exotic flowers. It forms a substantial bush with beautiful leaves; they arch elegantly and are up to 9in/23cm long, narrow, pointed, mid-green with pronounced veins. The flowers in June are purple-red tubes, paler at the centre, held in bold swooping panicles up to 8in/20cm long. In all but the most favoured gardens it must have the protection of a wall and a sunny position. It flowers on the previous season's growth so it may only be pruned after flowering. It may be propagated by cuttings.

Of all the buddlejas I like this the best. Its foliage is beautiful – soft pale grey-green leaves, 2in/5cm long, pointed and slightly toothed, borne on felty new growth. The leaves flutter easily in the breeze revealing their silvery white undersides. The flowers appear in late May but continue for many weeks, the very palest lilac-coloured panicles with a rich honeyed scent. It needs a warm and sunny position and may successfully be trained against a wall where its lovely foliage will mingle easily with clematises and the smaller roses. I grow it on a high wall behind *Lavatera* 'Barnsley', with

whose pale pink flowers the lilac and grey of the buddleja harmonize beautifully. It should be pruned in March, back to the main woody framework, which will stimulate new growth on which the flowers are borne. It is easy to propagate from cuttings.

Bupleurum

There are about 100 species of bupleurum, woody and herbaceous, in the family Umbelliferae, native to South Africa, Asia, North America and Europe.

Bupleurum fruticosum
Origin: S. Europe
Height: 8ft/2.5m
Z: 7

❧ The foliage of this evergreen shrub is, in form and colour, a perpetual garden ornament. The leaves are leathery, narrow, slightly rounded but coming to a point, and up to 5in/13cm long. The upper side of the leaves is glistening grey-green but the underside, revealed as they toss in the wind, is the palest grey. The flowers start in July and last many weeks, delicate umbels of diminutive yellow buttons, held airily aloft on fleshy glaucous new stems with a purple-brown bloom. It forms a spreading bush of rather lax growth but with quite enough character to make it a powerful presence in the mixed border. It is best in an open sunny position and it may be propagated by cuttings. Its shape may be improved by pruning gently in spring.

Buxus

There are about seventy species of this genus, all evergreen woody plants, in the family Buxaceae, widely distributed in Africa, East Asia, Central America and Europe.

Buxus sempervirens
Origin: Mediterranean
Height: 20ft/6m
Z: 6

In the wild, box will grow into a substantial shrub or small tree of striking sprawling habit. In the garden, however, it is almost invariably used for hedging or topiary, for which it is extremely valuable. The leaves, fresh lime-green when young, darkening to a fine deep green, are ¹/₂in/1.25cm long, oval and slightly twisted, giving off a pungent scent in the sun, which I love but many hate. It takes clipping (in summer) very well, forming a dense but lively texture, admirable for hedges where it should be planted 5in/12.5cm apart, in sun or shade, in rich soil. The dwarf box, *B.s.* 'Suffruticosa', has very small leaves and lends itself excellently to low edging for paths or borders. Both are easily propagated by cuttings in summer which, although slow to root, are very reliable.

Camellia

There are about eighty species of camellia, in the family Theaceae, native to eastern Asia, which include the tea plant, *C. sinensis*. These evergreen shrubs or bushy trees produce some of the most exquisite flowers of any plant, and many camellias also have very handsome glossy leaves. However, from the gardener's point of view they present major problems. They are at their best in an exceptionally mild humid

Camellia 'Rosea Superba'

climate and rich acid soil, which few gardens enjoy. Many flower in late winter, when all but the most favoured gardens will experience frost; this discolours flowers or kills buds. Many, too, have a rather lax and sprawling habit which looks awkward in formal gardens, though perfectly acceptable in a wilder woodland setting. A carefully chosen and well sited camellia can look wonderful in a garden – or in a large pot – and although camellias in general cannot be recommended for the majority of gardens, if you do possess the right soil and climate, you will want to fill your garden with camellias and will need information and recommendations beyond the scope of this book.

Carpenteria

A genus of one species only in the family Hydrangeaceae/Philadelphaceae, native to California.

Carpenteria californica
Origin: California
Height: 8ft/2.4m
Z: 8

🌣 In all but the warmest gardens this distinguished evergreen shrub needs the protection of a wall. The mid-green slightly shiny leaves are slim but rounded, 4in/10cm long. The flowers appear in June and are very profuse – striking, single, white, 2¹/₂in/6cm across, with warm yellow anthers. After the flowers have fallen the new growth has striking purple-black stems. It forms a rather lax shapeless bush but in the border it may be buttressed by sturdier plantings through which its flower branches may weave; otherwise it can be successfully trained against the wall.

Carpenteria californica

Caryopteris

*Caryopteris ×
clandonensis*
Origin: Garden
Height: 3ft/1m
Z: 8

There are fifteen species of caryopteris, in the family Verbenaceae, all native to east Asia.

❧ This late-flowering aromatic deciduous shrub is very valuable in the border. The elegant toothed leaves of a handsome grey-green, smelling strongly of varnish when crushed or brushed, make a very good background to soft pinks and blues. In late summer the flowers appear, lively lavender-blue tufts, lasting well to the first frosts of autumn. It does best in a sunny dry position and thrives in poor soil. It should be firmly pruned in early spring before growth starts, which will both promote flowering and keep the bush shapely. It is very easily propagated from cuttings. There are two cultivars often seen in gardens: 'Heavenly Blue' makes a more compact bush and 'Kew Blue' has especially rich blue flowers.

Ceanothus

Ceanothus arboreus
'Trewithen Blue'
Origin: Garden
Height: 20ft/6m
Z: 8

Ceanothus × delileanus
'Gloire de Versailles'
Origin: Garden
Height: 12ft/3.6m
Z: 7

There are about fifty species of ceanothus, all woody, in the family Rhamnaceae, and all native to North America. Ceanothus enthusiasts want to possess them all but few are really outstanding garden plants.

❧ This evergreen ceanothus has much larger and more distinguished foliage than most of the tribe. The leaves are rounded, up to 3in/8cm long, slightly toothed and of an excellent gleaming dark green. The flowers in May or June are a rich blue, only slightly scented, and carried in bold panicles up to 4in/10cm long. It must have a sheltered position and will need wall protection in all but the warmest gardens. Above all it should be shielded from icy spring winds. It should not be overfed or it will produce an excess of foliage at the expense of flowers. It may be propagated by cuttings.

❧ An evergreen shrub, this too may be successfully trained against a sunny wall where its exceptional flowers and decorative foliage can intermingle with climbing plants. The leaves are a fresh green, narrow toothed shapely ovals, up to 3in/8cm long. The

flowers in July or August are a wonderful soft pale blue, carried in bottle-brush heads up to 2in/5cm long. They are borne on the current season's growth and plants should be pruned hard back (to two leaf-buds) in March. It looks beautiful with a second flush of the flowers of the pink rose 'Zéphirine Drouhin' and I grow the ghostly white viticella clematis 'Alba Luxurians' with it. It may be propagated by cuttings.

Ceratostigma

There are eight species of ceratostigma, all woody plants, in the family Plumbaginaceae, native to Africa and Asia.

Ceratostigma willmottianum
Origin: China, Tibet
Height: 30in/75cm
Z: 7

❧ There is nothing flashy or obvious about this small deciduous shrub, but it exudes distinction in every detail. The leaves are mid-green, a gracefully rounded oval, pointed at each end, up to 2¹/₂in/6cm long, with margins glistening with very fine hairs. The flowers appear in July, opening from tassle-like buds, and continue for weeks. They are single, of a brilliant sky-blue, paler towards the centre, no more than ¹/₂in/1.25cm across but carried in generous bunches at the ends of stems. The leaves are extremely ornamental, turning in autumn a rich red-brown, when the plant is still in flower. In all but the mildest gardens the top growth will be cut back in winter frosts and it behaves, in effect, like a herbaceous plant. The dead growth, bearing spiked seed-heads, should be cut back in early spring to form a handsomely rounded bush. It does well in part-shade or full sun, and in poor soil, and may be propagated by cuttings.

Choisya

This is a genus of a single species belonging to the family Rutaceae.

Choisya ternata
Origin: Mexico
Height: 6ft/1.8m
Z: 8

❧ This evergreen shrub is sometimes called Mexican orange blossom and its single white flowers against the rich green foliage do resemble an orange tree but without, alas, the delicious scent. The shiny rounded foliage is very ornamental and it has an attractive pungent scent when bruised. It forms a fine billowing plant, as wide as its height in time, giving admirable shape to a sunny border where it will thrive in any except waterlogged soil. The flowers are borne in profusion from April onwards, a cheerful sight against the dark green leaves. It can be clipped into shape after flowering and is easily propagated by cuttings. There is a new cultivar, 'Sundance', with yellow foliage which I do not like at all; it looks permanently diseased and has none of the sparkling vitality of the type.

Cistus

There are about twenty species of cistus, in the family Cistaceae, all evergreen shrubs, native to the Mediterranean countries. They are not long-lived and all may be propagated by cuttings. No cistus should be pruned into old wood; newer growth may be lightly clipped to shape in spring. All need sharp drainage, light soil and plenty of sunshine.

Cistus × corbariensis
Origin: S. Europe
Height: 5ft/1.5m
Z: 7

❧ The combination of colours and textures makes this cistus exceptionally garden worthy. The leaves are pale green, felty, crinkled at the edges when first opening, and maturing to 2in/5cm long heart shapes. The flower buds, fully formed in May, are decorative – plump, pointed and rosy pink, hanging slightly downwards. The flowers open in June, silky white, 1½in/4cm across, with striking yellow centres. It makes a compact rounded bush, a shapely presence in the border.

Cistus × corbariensis

Cistus × cyprius
Origin: Garden
Height: 6ft/1.8m
Z: 7

❧ There are several kinds of cistus that have white flowers with dashing deep maroon spots at the base of the petals; this is one of the very best. The leaves are very handsome and unusually large, dark green, up to 3in/8cm long and exuding aromatic gum which has a spicy varnish-like scent. The single flowers are up to 3in/8cm across, a crisp papery white with very deep red splotches at the foot of the petals. Among the larger of the tribe, it will contribute bold structure to a corner of a sunny border.

Cistus × cyprius

Cistus × purpureus
Origin: Garden
Height: 4ft/1.2m
Z: 7

❧ This is one of the hardier cistuses with some of the best flowers. The leaves are grey-green, aromatic, up to 2in/5cm long. The flowers in June, carried very profusely, are single, unusually large, up to 3in/8cm across, and a wonderful rich silvery mauve-pink with deeper spots of colour at the base of the petals. It is a superb border plant, looking marvellous with the gentle blues of campanulas.

Convolvulus

There are about 250 species of convolvulus, herbaceous and woody, in the family Convolvulaceae, very widely distributed in the warmer regions of Africa, Asia, America and Europe. They include the lovely but alarming European bindweed, *Convolvulus arvensis*, which only the boldest gardener would introduce into the garden. For the herbaceous species see pages 91–92.

Convolvulus cneorum
Origin: N. Africa,
S. Europe
Height: 12in/30cm
Z: 8

❧ Few plants have such exquisite foliage as this. The leaves are very narrow, 1in/2.5cm long, a wonderful pale silver like newly polished pewter. The flowers in June are scarcely less attractive – single, white, 1¹/₂in/4cm across, slightly funnel-shaped with delicately pleated petals and yellow anthers. The profuse buds are tipped with pink before opening. It is essential to give it a sunny very well-drained position where it will be at home among other plants of Mediterranean character. It is not at all long-lived and should be propagated by cuttings.

Corylopsis

There are about twenty species of corylopsis, in the witch hazel family, Hamamelidaceae, native to China and Japan. The one described below is not showy but is nonetheless a shrub of distinctive beauty.

Corylopsis pauciflora
Origin: Japan
Height: 6ft/2m
Z: 6

❧ This has something of the character of a witch hazel but the form of the flowers is more beautiful. They appear in March, dangling on the leafless branches, wax-textured, cream-yellow, bell-shaped, 1in/2.5cm long, emerging from calyces tinged with pink. Despite its specific name (which means 'few flowers') it will flower profusely, making an exquisite cloud of the softest yellow which looks marvellous with pale blue – of, for example, *Chionodoxa luciliae*. The foliage, rounded, heart-shaped and elegantly pleated, is flushed with pink when it first appears. It forms a spreading

Illustration opposite:
Cotoneaster horizontalis

open bush – a pair flanking a gate or opening makes a fine garden ornament even when not in flower. It needs a protected slightly shaded position in moist soil and will not tolerate chalk.

Cotinus

Cotinus coggygria 'Royal Purple'
Origin: Garden (China, S. Europe)
Height: 9ft/2.75m
Z: 6

There are three species of cotinus, in the family Anacardiaceae, native to North America, southern Europe and Asia.

❧ This purple-leaved form of the smoke tree is a very handsome and versatile border shrub. The leaves, rounded and up to 3in/8cm long, are reddish-purple when young, maturing to a deep chocolatey purple with a wonderful soft texture, as though made of the finest silk velvet. The flowers, insignificant little dirty yellow stars appearing in June, have infinitesimally fine silky branchlets, giving the plant in July the appearance of being enveloped in smoke. It likes a sunny position and does well in poor soil. Use it repeated in a border to give powerful structure and provide a background to other plantings. It may be propagated by cuttings.

Cotoneaster

There are at least seventy species of cotoneaster, in the family Rosaceae, native to North Africa, Asia and Europe. Most of these are rather dull plants with little to recommend them to gardeners except for cheerful berries and fine autumn colour in some

instances. To those qualities the one species described below adds striking habit of growth. Cotoneasters are susceptible to fireblight and affected branches should be removed and burnt.

Cotoneaster horizontalis
Origin: China
Height: 36in/90cm
Z: 4

❧ This deciduous shrub has unique fishbone-like branches which spread horizontally across the ground in bold sweeps. The leaves are a gleaming dark green, oval and up to $^1/_2$in/1.25cm long, which are shown to advantage by the little white flowers in spring. They colour very late in the autumn to spectacular shades of orange-red and in winter the decorative fruit, like diminutive apples, are a very cheerful glistening red. If you have the room, a pair looks magnificent flanking an entrance or fringing the pedestal of some statue or garden ornament. Apart from its susceptibility to fireblight, it is a very tough long-lived plant. It is easily propagated by cuttings.

Cytisus

There are about seventy species of cytisus, in the family Leguminosae, native to the Mediterranean countries and central Europe.

Cytisus battandieri
Origin: N. Africa
Height: 15ft/4.5m
Z: 7

❧ The Moroccan broom has exceptionally beautiful foliage. Each leaf is up to 3in/8cm long, rounded, a fine silvery grey-green, even paler on the underside, which is attractively revealed as branches flutter in the wind. The flowers, in late May, are a rich lemon-yellow, upright racemes 5in/13cm long, with a strong sweetly astringent scent, a mixture of pineapple and lemon. Vigorous young plants will throw out new branches 36–48in/90cm–120cm long, and may be kept in order by cutting back the previous year's growth by two-thirds after flowering. I grow it as a free-standing bush in a position of semi-shade. In the wild it flourishes in poor stony soil, which seems to produce paler foliage than rich soil. In colder places it may benefit from being trained against a wall but it is impossible to keep it both neat *and* floriferous. It is propagated by cuttings or by seed.

Daphne

There are about seventy species of daphne, in the family Thymelaeaceae, whose native habitats range widely from Asia and Australia to Europe.

Daphne odora 'Aureomarginata'

Daphne odora
Origin: China
Height: 36in/90cm
Z: 8

ﻬ This evergreen daphne is well named for it has fabulously scented flowers which alone would earn its place in the garden – the perfume of honeysuckle but with heavily spicy overtones. The buds appear in late winter, rich deep purple, opening into clusters of very small white flowers with pointed petals. The variety most commonly seen is *D.o.* 'Aureomarginata', with lightly variegated foliage, supposedly rather hardier than the type. It has an exotic presence in the garden, and the leaves are leathery, slightly wavy and pointed, marked with irregular paler margins. In full flower in late March or April, its heady scent fills the air. In a sheltered sunny corner with plenty of nourishment it will grow slowly to form a sprawling bush of character. It should not be pruned but may be propagated by cuttings.

Daphne retusa
Origin: China
Height: 24in/60cm
Z: 7

❧ With its handsome evergreen foliage, compact form and good flowers this is a very valuable shrub for the smaller garden. The leaves are glistening green, 2in/5cm long, and make a fine background to the rich deep purple flower buds which fatten up in March to open in April into clusters of the palest pink single star-shaped flowers with a richly perfumed scent. The bark is of a particularly fine cinnamon colour. It will grow quite slowly, always maintaining a well-rounded compact habit, and will flourish in half shade or full sun. I grow it in a shady place among pale primulas.

Deutzia

There are about fifty species of deutzia, in the family Hydrangeaceae, distributed in Asia, the Himalayas and Central America. Many have pretty little flowers but are in other respects rather unexciting plants.

Deutzia × rosea
'Campanulata'
Origin: Garden
Height: 36in/90cm
Z: 6

❧ Of the many deutzias bred by the French nurseryman Lemoine at the turn of the century this is one I like best. The leaves unfurl in April, 3in/8cm long, pointed, finely serrated, and varying in width from the slender to the curvaceously oval. The prolific flower buds are a chocolate colour and open into single white flowers touched with pink 1in/2.5cm across, with chocolate calyces and stems. The contrast is very elegant and the bush has an emphatic upright character. It flowers on old wood so any pruning to shape must be done soon after flowering. It likes a sunny position and may be propagated by cuttings.

Dorycnium

There are fifteen species of dorycnium, in the family Leguminosae, native to the Mediterranean region.

Dorycnium hirsutum
Origin: Mediterranean
Height: 18in/45cm
Z: 8

❧ The great virtue of this little evergreen shrub is the colour and texture of its leaves. They are pale grey, quite small, and of a very soft woolly texture. The flowers from June onwards contribute to its ghostly character. They are borne rather sparsely, creamy grey with a hint of pink, diminutive tubes with lipped openings. The seed changes in colour from brown-red to a decorative shining black, and in an appropriate place it will seed itself modestly. It forms a rather floppy but distinctive plant which must have a sunny position and good drainage; it will do well in rather poor and stony soil. Its shape may be improved by giving it a firm pruning in spring. It is not long-lived but is very easily propagated by seed.

Drimys

There are about thirty-five species of drimys, in the family Winteraceae, all from South America and Australasia.

Drimys winteri
Origin: S. Chile
Height: 12ft/3.6m
Z: 8

❧ This is an evergreen shrub of the greatest beauty, that demands a sunny sheltered position. The leaves are 6in/15cm long, narrow and slightly pointed, grey-green above and pale grey beneath. The new shoots bearing these leaves are a fine dusty purple. The flowers appear in May, a profusion of small white stars with striking

green-yellow stamens, opening from wax-like white spheres. At the back of a deep border, protected by a high wall, drimys gives unique character. Reference books invariably claim that the flowers are scented; while I was writing this book I stuck my nose deeply into the flowers of four specimens in different gardens and could smell nothing at all.

Elaeagnus

Elaeagnus commutata
Origin: North America
Height: 10ft/3m
Z: 2

This is a genus of about forty species, in the family Elaeagnaceae, whose native habitats are in North America, eastern Asia and southern Europe.

❧ This is a true aristrocrat among deciduous shrubs, with exceptionally beautiful foliage that provides an excellent background to other plantings. The leaves, emerging in April, are narrow and pointed, 2in/5cm long, of the palest silvery grey; it is the nearest thing to the foliage of the olive tree that may be grown in colder gardens. In May or June very small rather insignificant yellow trumpet-shaped flowers open to release a heady honeyed scent that travels across the garden. It has no special requirements as to soil and will grow well in light shade where its grey foliage has a particularly ghostly presence. In my garden shoots of the silvery pink rose 'New Dawn' followed by the deep purple clematis 'Etoile de Violette', intermingle with it to dazzling effect. It may be propagated by cuttings or by digging up a sucker. There is a variety, of uncertain origin, called 'Caspica', that has even paler foliage.

Enkianthus

There are ten species of enkianthus, in the family Ericaceae, all from eastern Asia.

Enkianthus campanulatus
Origin: Japan
Height: 10ft/3m
Z: 5

❧ This deciduous shrub has elegant little leaves, 1¹/₂in/4cm long, with finely serrated margins, borne on reddish new growth. The flowers open in May, a spectacular cascade of hanging bell shapes, ¹/₂in/1.25cm long, cream-coloured but suffused with rosy veins. It forms an open spreading bush, a fresh green throughout the summer but turning brilliant red in the autumn. It needs a moist acid soil and will do well in semi-shade. It is a shrub of great character and varied effects, that looks marvellous at the back of a large shady border. It may be propagated by cuttings.

Escallonia

There are about fifty species of escallonia, in the family Escalloniaceae, all woody, native to South America. None is very hardy in cold gardens and only one, in my view, is truly worth the trouble.

Escallonia 'Iveyi'
Origin: Garden
Height: 8ft/2.5m
Z: 9

❧ This evergreen shrub has very beautiful foliage set off in summer by a dazzling display of flowers. The leaves are dark green, glistening, and very finely toothed, elegantly rounded and up to 2in/5cm long. In July the flowers open, profuse bunches of little white tubes whose bases are flushed with pale pink, giving off a faint sweet scent. In a generous border it will provide permanent decoration, its glossy foliage sparkling with light at any time of year. It must have a protected, warm position: the south-west corner of walls or hedges is ideal. In severe winters established plants, even if cut to the ground, will in all likelihood grow from the base; it is vulnerable to spring frosts but will recover. It may be lightly pruned in late spring to keep a good shape and may be propagated by cuttings.

Exochorda

Exochorda × macrantha
'The Bride'
Origin: Garden
Height: 5ft/1.5m
Z: 5

There are five species of exochorda, in the family Rosaceae, native to central and eastern Asia.

❧ This is a valuable deciduous flowering shrub for the smaller garden. It makes a rounded compact bush with rather lax branches bearing pale green foliage, becoming darker as the season progresses. The flowers appear in May, when a great profusion of creamy white buds open into lavish racemes of single white flowers, 1¹/₂in/4cm across, with marked lime-green stamens. It is equally at home in sun or part shade, and will not tolerate limy soil. It may be propagated by cuttings.

Fothergilla

Fothergilla major
Origin: E. North America
Height: 8ft/2.4m
Z: 5

There are two species of fothergilla, in the family Hamamelidaceae, both native to eastern North America.

❧ This compact deciduous shrub performs handsomely in two seasons and is full of character. The leaves open in March, rounded, gently pleated and delicately toothed, 3in/8cm long. The flowers open in April or May, a profusion of greenish-white puffs

1¹/₂in/4cm long, giving off a mysterious sweet scent. In autumn the foliage turns brilliant colours from tawny yellow to crimson-purple – a most spectacular sight and among the best of all autumn foliage colours. It likes a rich lime-free humus and a position in semi-shade or sun. It may be propagated by cuttings.

Fothergilla major

Garrya

Garrya elliptica
Origin: W. North America
Height: 15ft/4.5m
Z: 9

There are eighteen species of this genus, in the family Garryaceae, all native to western North America.

❧ This evergreen shrub has very fine grey-green oval leaves with undulating margins and slightly toothed, 2–3in/5–8cm long, making a sombre but distinguished background to more colourful planting. The flowers on male plants are in the form of spectacular pale grey catkins 6in/10cm long (even longer in warmer places), a brilliant winter ornament, appearing between November and January. The catkins on female plants are much shorter but there is a cultivar, male only, *G.e.* 'James Roof', with the biggest catkins of all, up to 14in/35cm long. It needs a warm position in all but the most favoured gardens. I have seen it filling a sunny

Garrya elliptica

corner, with *Rosa glauca* in front, the purplish-grey foliage and rich pink flowers marvellous against the sombre grey of the garrya.

Hydrangea

Hydrangea aspera villosa
(syn. *H. villosa*)
Origin: China
Height: 12ft/3.6m
Z: 7

There are about 100 species of these evergreen and deciduous woody plants, in the family Hydrangeaceae, native to the Americas and Asia.

❧ The foliage of this deciduous hydrangea is especially distinguished. Each leaf is up to 6in/15cm long, oval, pointed and slightly toothed, mid-green and downy with a much paler underside. The intricate flower buds, flushed with pink, are carried at the tips of stems and open in July in spectacular corymbs of rosy mauve flowers, each 1¹/₂in/4cm across. It will do well in a position of semi-shade or in full sun. It may be propagated by cuttings. It will make a substantial stately bush, too large for many gardens, but can be kept in control by pruning, as hard as you like, in late spring. In this way it may be used as an excellent border plant, giving great beauty of foliage and spectacular flower colour when other border stalwarts are flagging. I grow it in a sea of pink Japanese anemone which flowers at the same time.

Illustration opposite:
Hydrangea aspera villosa

Hydrangea quercifolia
Origin: S.E. North America
Height: 7ft/2m
Z: 5

❧ The beautiful foliage is the most memorable thing about this distinguished deciduous shrub. The leaves are boldly shaped, distinctly oak-like as the name suggests, rounded, fresh pale green, up to 6in/15cm across, with pointed lobes and a soft felty surface. They point in different directions, giving a feeling of movement and liveliness. The new growth, on which the leaves are carried, is a fine golden tawny colour. In July spires of creamy white flowers up to 8in/20cm long appear, not dramatic but handsome and distinguished. The autumn colour is brilliant, ranging from orange to deep purple. A variety with double flowers, *H.q.* 'Snowflake', has a generously blowsy air to it. It is best in rich soil in sun or semi-shade.

Ilex

Ilex aquifolium
Origin: N. Africa, Asia
Minor, Europe
Height: 45ft/15m
Z: 7

There are about 400 species of holly, in the family Aquifoliaceae, very widely distributed in tropical and temperate regions.

❧ The English holly is immensely long-lived and will grow slowly to form a superb middle-sized tree with wonderfully decorative pale grey bark. For garden purposes it is best known as a shrub that takes clipping very well, and may be used for simple topiary or

Ilex aquifolium 'Golden van Tol'

hedging. The evergreen leaves, 3in/8cm long, are very deep glossy green, with scalloped margins and sharp spines. In very old specimens the leaf becomes more regular in shape and less thorny. In late autumn the brilliant scarlet berries appear, to last, if not eaten by birds, through the winter. Both female and male forms are needed for berries to be produced. It is undemanding as to soil or site, doing well even in dry shade where its glistening foliage is very decorative. It makes an excellent garden hedge with a lively texture and is an effective ingredient for a mixed 'tapestry' hedge with, for example, beech (*Fagus sylvatica*) and copper beech (*F.s. purpurea*). Plants should be spaced 24in/60cm apart and clipped in spring or autumn. It is very easy to propagate from seed and has given rise to large numbers of cultivars of which *I.a.* 'J.C. van Tol' is especially valuable, with handsomely rounded leaves and fewer spikes. There are many variegated cultivars, some of which provide a cheerful presence on a winter's day; others are so strident that they do not fit easily into the garden. *I.a* 'Golden Milkboy' is a good one with fine pale yellow leaves edged with green; *I.a.* 'Ferox Argentea' bristles with spines and has narrow pale yellow margins; *I.a.* 'Golden van Tol' has sumptuous gold edges.

Ilex myrtifolia
Origin: S. North America
Height: 8ft/2.5m
Z: 8

❧ This is a very attractive holly for the smaller garden. It has very narrow elegant toothed leaves, 1 ¹/₂in/4cm long, a good rich dark green which contrasts decoratively with the paler young growth in spring. Its small leaves take clipping well, and it makes an unusual but very handsome plant for topiary. It naturally forms a pyramid shape and unclipped plants, with their emphatically shapely form, are excellent in the border, consorting well with other plantings and giving winter interest and structure. It has no particular demands of soil but does like a warm position. It is easily propagated by cuttings.

Itea

There are ten species of itea, deciduous and evergreen trees and shrubs, in the family Iteaceae, native to North America and Asia.

Itea ilicifolia
Origin: China
Height: 10ft/3m
Z: 7

❧ This evergreen shrub has distinguished foliage and striking flowers in late summer. The leaves, as the name suggests, are like a holly, but vary considerably; they are rounded, up to 2¹/₂in/6cm long, slightly toothed. When young they are a fresh glistening green but become darker, though no less distinguished, with age. The flowers appear in July or August, elegant hanging racemes to 12in/30cm long, composed of countless diminutive flowers which turn from lime-green to creamy white. It does best in a north-facing but protected site; here, in the shade, its beautiful gleaming foliage is seen to full advantage. It may be propagated by cuttings.

Laurus

There are two species in this genus, in the family Lauraceae, both of which are native to southern Europe and the Canary Islands.

Laurus nobilis
Origin: S. Europe
Height: 10ft/3m
Z: 9

❧ The sweet bay, whose dried leaves produce one of the essential culinary herbs, is a beautiful evergreen shrub much used in warmer countries like Italy as an admirable hedging material. The leaves are a slender oval, up to 5in/12.5cm long, pointed at each end and with undulating edges. Deep glistening green, they make an outstanding background to other planting, and clipped specimens in a warm border give ornament and structure. The stems are a handsome reddish-black and creamy insignificant flowers in early spring produce shining black berries. This is not a plant for an exposed site in a cold garden but it has no special soil requirements. It may be propagated easily by seed or by cuttings.

Lavandula

There are about twenty-five species of lavender, in the family Labiatae, native to southern Europe and as far east as India.

Lavandula angustifolia
Origin: S. Europe
Height: 24in/60cm
Z: 6

❧ Common lavender is a marvellous aromatic evergreen shrub which should not be overlooked merely because it is common. The slender, dense and upright-growing grey-green foliage is very ornamental, and in sun or when brushed, gives off the characteristic delicious gummy scent. The flowers, like narrow brushes 2in/5cm long, open in May or June and range in colour from pale, almost white, to deep blue-violet, heavily scented. It makes a very attractive low hedge, short-lived but easily propagated by cuttings. It is always at its best in light soil in a sunny position. To keep a well-rounded shape plants may be pruned hard in early spring. An especially good cultivar is *L.a.* 'Hidcote', with broader pointed very pale leaves and deep violet flowers.

Lavandula stoechas

Lavandula stoechas
Origin: S. Europe
Height: 18in/45cm
Z: 8

❧ French lavender is tender and needs a well-drained site in a sunny position, but it is well worth the care. The evergreen leaves are pale grey, very narrow, while the flowers in May are wonderfully exotic – like miniature pineapples but deep blue-purple below, with tufts of pale violet petal-like bracts above. All parts of the plant have a piercing varnish-like aroma which, in full sun, wafts across the garden. It is very easily propagated by cuttings. A subspecies, *L.s. pedunculata*, has much longer upper bracts, a fine indigo blue, that twist sideways and are extremely ornamental.

Lavatera

There are twenty-five species of lavatera, woody and herbaceous, in the family Malvaceae, very widely distributed in North America, Asia, Australasia and Europe.

Lavatera 'Barnsley'
Origin: Garden
Height: 8ft/2.5m
Z: 8

❧ The naming of this semi-shrubby plant has caused botanists much agony but gardeners need have no doubt of its charm. It grows very quickly to form a bush of fleshy growth with purple stems and handsome soft pale green leaves with three slightly pointed lobes, up to 4in/10cm long. The flowers, starting in June, are borne prolifically right through the growing season until the first frosts. They are single, very pale pink, fading almost to white, with a red eye, 2½in/6cm across. It makes an excellent substantial border shrub where a sunny position and rich soil will suit it best. Flowering on new growth, it may be pruned as hard as you like in the spring to keep it to size. It is very shallow-rooted and large specimens will certainly need support. Although short-lived it is very easily propagated by cuttings.

Magnolia

There are about eighty species of magnolia, in the family Magnoliaceae, distributed in eastern North America, eastern Asia and the Himalayas. These are among the most widely admired of all flowering shrubs and every gardener should find room for one or two.

Magnolia × *soulangeana*
Origin: Garden
Height: 18ft/6m
Z: 5

❧ This hybrid is one of the commonest flowering shrubs for the perfectly good reason that it is extremely beautiful and very easy to cultivate. It has two great ornamental qualities: its flowers and its elegant shape. The flowers, with waxy petals, 6in/15cm long, are pure white but smudged with purple on the outside, and borne on the leafless stems in great profusion – a tremendously exhilarating sight. They open in April from large upward-pointing candle-like buds. As the foliage appears, a fresh lime-green, attention is drawn to the spreading form of the shrub, often as wide as it is high. It needs rich moist soil and a sunny position protected from cold winds. In the garden it is often used to striking effect as a specimen on a lawn. It is wonderful underplanted with spring bulbs – *Anemone blanda*, crocuses, *Cyclamen coum* and snowdrops. There are many cultivars but none with quite the distinction of the original.

Magnolia stellata
Origin: Japan
Height: 10–15ft/3–4.5m
Z: 4

❧ You would have to be a stony-hearted gardener to resist the charms of this flowering shrub. The flower buds start to fatten up in the winter and, long before they open, become attractive ornaments in themselves – slender and glistening with silver down. As the buds open in March they are tinged with a creamy pink but

Illustration opposite:
Magnolia × *soulangeana*

the flowers themselves, borne in great clouds, are a dazzling white, 4in/10cm across when fully open, with many slim strap-shaped petals and a heady scent of primroses. The foliage appears after the flowers: pale green with rounded leaves. It is not particular as regards soil – I have seen it growing equally well in deep acid soil and on chalk, but it will respond well to lavish feeding and must have an open position. It is a slow-growing shrub of an upright rounded habit with distinctive presence suitable for the border or as a specimen on a lawn. Its light foliage means that plants may be grown underneath: sheets of the silvery marbled foliage of *Cyclamen hederifolium* look fabulous, or a group of the creamy white tulip, *Tulipa fosteriana* 'Purissima'. There is a cultivar, *M.s.* 'Rosea', with particularly good warm pink flowers.

Mahonia

There are about ninety species of mahonia, in the family Berberidaceae, all native to North and Central America and Asia.

Mahonia aquifolium
Origin: N.W. North America
Height: 5ft/1.5m
Z: 5

❧ The Oregon grape is not as obviously glamorous as its Asiatic cousins but it has admirable qualities for the smaller garden. Its holly-like foliage, pinnate with prickly leaflets, is a dark glossy green which often takes on handsome bronze tints. The tresses of tiny flowers appearing in March or April are a handsome deep gold and give off a sweet scent. The fruit, which give the plant its common name, are splendid – black dusted with an attractive bloom, hanging in a good year in profuse and highly decorative bunches. It is often used in large gardens as ground-cover but I like to see it as a free-standing bush, excellent in a border where its sombre but gleaming foliage is an excellent foil in summer to brighter plantings. It is undemanding as to soil and grows well in shade. It is propagated by seeds or by cuttings.

Mahonia × media

Mahonia × media
Origin: Garden
Height: 10ft/3m
Z: 8

❧ This is a stately and magnificent evergreen shrub, a hybrid between two Asiatic mahonias, but unfortunately rather tender. The pinnate leaves are very large, up to 24in/60cm long, carried on arching branches. The primrose-yellow flowers appear in winter, carried above the foliage in generous plumes 18in/45cm tall; they are intensely fragrant, resembling the scent of lily-of-the-valley. The new foliage in the spring is a striking mahogany in colour. It will do well shaded under a light canopy of trees and larger shrubs, which will also afford some frost protection, and likes a rich moist soil. This is not at all a plant for the border but for ornamental woodland where its bold foliage and deliciously scented flowers give it unique presence. It is found in several excellent cultivars: 'Buckland', 'Charity' and 'Lionel Fortescue'. It may be propagated by cuttings.

Myrtus

There are two species of myrtles, in the family Myrtaceae, native to the Mediterranean region.

Myrtus communis
Origin: Mediterranean
Height: 15ft/4.5m
Z: 8

❧ The common myrtle is not a remotely showy plant, but quite apart from its classical and romantic associations has irresistible charm. It is evergreen, with dense foliage of shapely glistening pointed leaves up to 2in/5cm long, which taking clipping very well; in Mediterranean countries it is used to make beautiful hedges. The flowers, in June or July, are white, single, rounded, 3/4in/2cm across with an emphatic explosion of white stamens at the centre, and a sweet but fugitive scent. The bark of older specimens is golden and has an attractive flaking texture. It forms a tall billowing bush and because of its admirable architectural character, a pair make a marvellous frame to an entrance. It needs a warm sunny position and may be propagated by cuttings.

Osmanthus

Osmanthus × burkwoodii
(x *Osmarea burkwoodii*)
Origin: Garden
Height: 7ft/2.1m
Z: 6

There are about fifteen species of osmanthus, in the family Oleaceae, found in south-east North America and eastern Asia.

❧ There are two good reasons for growing this distinguished evergreen shub – its fine foliage and a dazzling scented profusion of flowers in early spring. The leaves are elegantly pointed, up to 1¹/₂in/4cm long, with very fine teeth and of a beautiful rich glistening green. They take clipping well and plants may be shaped in late spring after flowering; they will make an hedge of particularly attractive texture and colour. The flowers, bunches of little white trumpets ¹/₂in/1.25cm long, at the tips of branches, have a sweet almond scent in the sun, which carries great distances – one of the best spring perfumes. Some plants form a single stem, or may be encouraged to do so, when they will resemble a very decorative miniature tree. Smaller climbers, such as *Clematis viticella*, look spectacular growing through the foliage in high summer. It is not at all choosy as regards soil and will do well in full sun or a partly shaded position.

Osmanthus × burkwoodii

Osmanthus heterophyllus
Origin: Japan
Height: 15ft/4.5m
Z: 7

❧ This evergreen shrub would make an excellent more sophisticated substitute for holly in a formal garden. The foliage is narrowly oval, elegantly toothed, 2¹/₂in/5cm long, and of a particularly handsome deep green. It has flowers very like those of *Osmanthus burkwoodii* and similarly fragrant, but they appear in

August or September. It may be clipped, and its fine glistening texture makes it excellent for hedging or topiary. A variegated form, *O.h.* 'Variegatus', has creamy margins to the leaves, without that bilious cast that spoils so many variegated plants. It is undemanding as to soil and will flourish in sun or semi-shade. It may be propagated by cuttings.

Paeonia

There are over thirty species of peony, in the family Paeoniaceae, most of which are herbaceous and are described on pages 138–41. The woody species are deciduous and come from China and Tibet.

Paeonia delavayi ludlowii
(P. lutea ludlowii)
Origin: Tibet
Height: 8ft/2.5m
Z: 6

❧ This Tibetan tree peony makes a subtantial shrub with magnificent leaves. They are deeply divided, up to 15in/35cm long, pale green and with a leathery texture. The single cupped flowers in May are a cool and beautiful yellow, 4in/10cm across, with elegantly frilled petals and a mass of anthers at the centre. It needs plenty of room, in a sunny position, and it flowers best in rather poor soil; soil that is too rich will produce excess foliage at the expense of flowers. It may be propagated by seed which is borne in decorative pods.

Paeonia delavayi ludlowii

Paeonia suffruticosa
Origin: China
Height: 6ft/1.8m
Z: 5

❧ The Moutan peony in flower is a breathtaking sight. The flowers unfold in May, generous and many-petalled, 6in/15cm across, white or pink. They are sweetly scented and carried on reddish stems above

Paeonia suffruticosa
'Reine Elizabeth'

bronze-flushed foliage. It is a superlative border plant, needing plenty of light to flower well. There are many cultivars of which *P.s.* 'Rock's Variety', with white flowers marked with deep maroon patches at the base, is a wonderful plant. Several very double white or pink kinds are available: *P.s.* 'Reine Elizabeth' is the palest pink, becoming red at the base of each petal. It may (with difficulty) be propagated by cuttings and nurserymen usually graft it.

Perovskia

There are seven species of perovskia, in the family Labiatae, native to Asia Minor, Central Asia and the Himalaya. They are all deciduous shrubs.

Perovskia abrotanoïdes
Origin: Afghanistan, Himalaya
Height: 4ft/1.2m
Z: 5

❧ The great virtues of this shrub, or subshrub, are its marvellous foliage and striking flowers produced late in the summer when few other plants are performing. The leaves are 2¹/₂in/6cm long, shaped like spearheads and slightly toothed, pointing elegantly upwards from almost white stems. The whole plant has an attractive

Perovskia atriplicifolia 'Blue Spire'

pungent resin-like aroma. In July curling spires of very small sky-blue flowers open at the tips of the stems – a beautiful contrast to the pale stems and the foliage. Flowers will continue throughout the autumn until the first frosts and the beauty of the plant continues even in winter when the leafless white stems make a lovely ornament. They should be cut down in early spring to encourage new growth. It likes a very sunny position and although it is said (like most plants) to need a well-drained site, I have grown it with perfect success in heavy clay. It may be propagated by cuttings. The more frequently seen *P. atriplicifolia* is similar in all respects to the above but it has deeply cut leaves with slightly wavy margins. A cultivar, *P. atriplicifolia* 'Blue Spire', has especially large flowers.

Philadelphus

There are sixty species of philadelphus, all woody, in the family Philadelphaceae, widely distributed in America and Asia. The overwhelming attraction of the genus is the delicious scent of their often very beautiful flowers, surely one of great summer perfumes. Their disadvantage, however, is that many of them form rather large and ungainly leafy shrubs which, when not in flower, contribute little. None of the species is a really valuable plant and it is only among the cultivars, of impenetrably complicated parentage, that we find outstanding examples. But even here many are embarrassingly large for all but the biggest gardens. I have chosen a few of the more modestly sized kinds, all with deliciously scented and beautiful flowers. The scent – peppery, intensely aromatic and sweet – is curiously imperceptible if you sniff the flower itself; it seems to catch one unawares in sudden heady gusts, especially in cool weather. All those described are hardy to Zone 6, flower in June and may be propagated by cuttings. They will flower best in an open position. There is no evidence that pruning encourages flowering but all may be shaped, and kept within bounds, by pruning after flowering.

Philadelphus 'Manteau
d'Hermine'

P. 'Belle Etoile' has large single white flowers, with markedly separate petals, 1¹/₂in/4cm across, and striking pink-purple centres with yellow anthers. It will form a bush up to 8ft/2.5m high. It has an especially pronounced scent. *P.* 'Beauclerk' is more vigorous than the above, up to 10ft/3m high. It has rounded, semi-double, creamy white flowers, 1¹/₂in/4cm across, with a pale purple mark at the centre. *P.* 'Manteau d'Hermine' is especially valuable for the smaller garden, growing no more than 4ft/1.2m. It has exquisite, very double white flowers, 1in/2.5cm across, lightly scented. It is in many ways the ideal small philadelphus, displaying in small size all the essential qualities of the genus.

Phlomis

Phlomis fruticosa
Origin: Mediterranean
Height: 6ft/1.8m
Z: 7

There are about 100 species of phlomis, woody and herbaceous, in the family Labiatae, native to Asia and southern Europe.

❧ The pale soft grey-white evergreen foliage of the Jerusalem sage, pungently scented, is wonderfully decorative. In late May or June its cheerful yellow flowers open, curious twisted whorls 2in/5cm across, looking well with the pale leaves. It requires a sunny well-drained position, and poor soil suits it well. In the border it has emphatic presence and may be clipped lightly to make a neater rounded shape; the dead flower heads should in any case be removed in late winter. It is very easily propagated by cuttings.

Phlomis fruticosa

Phlomis italica
Origin: Balearic Islands
Height: 36in/90cm
Z: 8

❧ This rather tender but beautiful evergreen shrub has pale grey leaves like little spearheads with rounded points, upward-pointing and up to 2in/5cm long. In June the flowers appear, whorls of delicate rosy mauve, each flower up to 3/4in/2cm. It must have a protected, sunny and well-drained site; heavy wet clay, especially in winter, will kill it. No other shrub with pale silvery leaves has the same flower colour as this and the combination is most decorative.

Pieris

There are about seven species of pieris, all evergreen woody plants, in the family Ericaceae, native to North America, Asia and the West Indies.

Pieris formosa forrestii
Origin: China
Height: 10ft/3m
Z: 7

❧ Some plants, beautiful in themselves, depend upon the right setting in the garden for their virtues to be properly revealed. This pieris, exotic and wild, looks silly in a border or constrained in some cramping corner. It is a woodland plant and it is in such a setting that it is seen at its best. The leathery evergreen leaves, up to 4in/10cm long, are a rich dark green, narrow and pointed, with a pronounced central rib. In March or April the new foliage emerges, upward-pointing plumes of startling red, easily mistaken in the distance for some brilliant flower. Simultaneous with the new foliage the flowers appear, hanging bunches of waxy creamy yellow bells, deliciously and intensely scented. It must have acid soil, and a protected position in semi-shade will prevent icy spring winds from damaging the tender new foliage. It may be propagated by cuttings. *P.f.f.* 'Wakehurst' has especially brilliant red new foliage and a widely seen hybrid, *P.* 'Forest Flame', has the additional virtue for colder gardens of coming into leaf a little later.

Pieris formosa forrestii
'Wakehurst'

Potentilla

Potentilla fruticosa
Origin: N. hemisphere
Height: 4ft/1.2m
Z: 3

There are about 500 species of potentilla, woody and herbaceous, in the family Rosaceae. For the herbaceous kinds see page 145.

❧ The species is rarely seen, and from the gardener's point of view the best plants are among the cultivars described below. The species is deciduous and makes a rounded neat bush with leaves of a silvery sheen, up to 1in/2.5cm long, and single rose-like flowers from May onwards, yellow or white, up to 1¹/₂in/4cm across. *P.f.* 'Katherine Dykes' has lovely clear primrose-

Potentilla fruticosa
'Katherine Dykes'

yellow flowers, 1in/2.5cm across, carried profusely, and grey-green foliage; *P. f.* 'Veitchii' is an especially good white-flowered variety, with larger flowers, 1¹/₂in/4cm across, and very good fresh green foliage. It grows a little larger than the type. *P. f.* 'Vilmoriniana' has exquisite pale creamy yellow flowers, 1¹/₂in/4cm across, with foliage of a marvellous silvery green. All these are beautiful small shrubs for the mixed border, with a long flowering season and with enough shapeliness and foliage interest to make handsome ornamental plants throughout the growing season. A light pruning in early spring (up to one third of the previous season's growth) will keep them in good shape. They may be propagated by cuttings.

Prunus

There are well over 400 species in this genus, in the family Rosaceae. Most are trees (including almonds, cherries and plums) and these are described in the section on pages 291–93.

Prunus × cistena
Origin: Garden
Height: 10ft/3m
Z: 3

❧ This American hybrid is an attractive deciduous shrub with handsome foliage and decorative spring blossom. In April, rich pink buds open into graceful single very pale pink flowers, ³/₄in/2cm across, which are shown to great advantage against the new foliage which emerges at the same time. The leaves are at first a fresh glistening reddish-brown; this becomes a more subdued purple later in the season when they provide an excellent background in the border to herbaceous plantings. It takes clipping well and does well in semi-shade where the pink flowers will be of a deeper colour. It has no particular requirements of soil and may be propagated from cuttings.

Prunus laurocerasus
Origin: E. Europe and Near East
Height: 15ft/4.5m
Z: 7

❧ The cherry laurel is a majestic evergreen shrub whose great virtues should not be overlooked just because it is common. It has magnificent glistening leaves, up to 6in/15cm long, slender, slightly toothed and pointed. Flowers appear in April, 5in/12.5cm tall upright candles formed of many diminutive creamy white flowers, giving off a dusty sweet scent. In late summer small black cherry-like fruit are borne, which birds feast on. It takes clipping well and forms an admirable bold hedge of informal character enlivened by the gleaming foliage. It is not choosy as to soil and may be propagated by suckers or by seed.

Prunus tenella
Origin: E. Europe
Height: 24in/60cm
Z: 2

❧ The Russian almond is a suckering low-growing shrub with wonderful pale pink spring flowers. It sends up single stems which happily thread through other plantings and in April are wreathed with single lively pink flowers, ¹/₂in/1.25cm across. The new foliage appears at the same time, a fresh green which later in the season is slightly flushed with pink. It will flower best in a sunny position, in any soil, and is very easily propagated by root division. It should be pruned hard after flowering to encourage new growth. It looks marvellous growing through the purple foliage of purple sage (*Salvia officinalis* 'Purpurascens') or other low growing shrubs of contrasting foliage. There is a cultivar, *P.t.* 'Fire Hill', larger and flashier than the type, and to my taste, entirely lacking its charm.

Rhododendron

Rhododendron luteum

This vast and immensely complicated genus has at least 500 species, in the family Ericaceae. By far the greatest number, and the most beautiful, come from Asia, although there are a few from North America and Europe.

From the point of view of the gardener, rhododendrons present problems. First, they are essentially limited to acid soil. Second, there has been a frenzied production of new cultivars, too many of which seem to clamour excessively for attention – like a film star with too much make up. Third, for my money, the species that seem to offer the essential rhododendron experience – the sort that bowl you over on sight – are the vast tree-like kinds such as *R. macabeanum* or *R. sinogrande*. These, with their beautiful evergreen foliage of gigantic size and spectacular flowers, really need a very mild humid climate where they will easily grow to form wide spreading trees at least 30ft/10m high. But these great rhododendron aristocrats look horribly ill-at-ease in any setting other than wild naturalistic woodland. However, if you are lucky enough to possess a large garden with the right climate and soil, few plants offer more pleasure. One further point: while the brilliant colour of many of the smaller rhododendrons, for example of the azalea group, will tend to overpower a border or command excessive attention in a smaller garden, in a woodland garden, glimpsed in the distance or half-veiled by other shrubs or trees, they can be brilliantly effective. The best I can do here is to pick out a few especially good examples from the smaller, easier species.

Rhododendron luteum
Origin: E. Europe
Height: 10ft/3m
Z: 5

❧ This deciduous azalea has several virtues that handsomely earn its place in the garden. The flowers open in May, five-petalled stars, 2in/5cm across, a pale golden-yellow with a deeper stripe on the inside of one of the petals. They have a wonderful scent, very sweet but with spicy undertones, which wafts great distances across the garden. The leaves are upwards-pointing, slender and downy, 2^{1}/$_{2}$in/6cm long, mid-green but flushed with a brownish-red; in autumn they colour a brilliant orange-red. It likes a sunny open position and is an excellent border plant, looking wonderful with *Euphorbia characias* and later in the season making an excellent support for herbaceous clematises such as *Clematis × durandii*. It self-seeds prolifically.

Rhododendron quinquefolium

*Rhododendron
quinquefolium*
Origin: Japan
Height: 7ft/2.1m
Z: 8

❧ This deciduous rhododendron combines exceptionally beautiful foliage with wonderfully delicate flowers. The lime-green leaves, as the name suggests, are arranged in fives, radiating from the stem, each leaf 2in/5cm long, rounded but with a point and exquisitely edged in rich red. The flowers open with the leaves in May, single white trumpets, 1in/2.5cm long. It is a slow-growing bush with an upright habit. It needs semi-shade, which may also provide some frost protection in colder places, and may successfully be underplanted with spring-flowering herbaceous plants; it looks wonderful with sheets of yellow-flowered *Uvularia grandiflora*.

*Rhododendron
williamsianum*

*Rhododendron
williamsianum*
Origin: China
Height: 4ft/1.2m
Z: 6

❧ Everything is harmonious about this compact evergreen rhododendron. It grows slowly to form a shapely rounded bush with rounded heart-shaped leaves, 1in/2.5cm long, mid-green above but the palest grey-green below, the colour of real pistachio ice-cream. The flowers, borne rather sparsely, appear in April. They are single, bell-shaped, 1¹/₂in/3.75cm long, a rich warm pink outside and very pale within. These are closely followed by the new foliage, a fine mahogany brown, which casts a reddish glow over the whole plant. Its distinctive shape makes it a valuable and versatile plant at all times of the year, as a punctuation mark in a border, or as a single specimen giving distinguished character to a corner of the garden.

Ribes

Ribes speciosum
Origin: California
Height: 7ft/2.1m
Z: 7

There are about 150 species of this genus, in the family Grossulariaceae, and they include the culinary blackcurrants and gooseberries.

❧ This decorative evergreen shrub, closely allied to the gooseberry, has very handsome rich green foliage of rounded lobed leaves carried on prickly stems; in hard winters its foliage may fall. In February the flower buds appear, a brilliant carmine against the green, and open out in late March, dangling tubes with protruding stamens like the antennae of an exotic insect, 1¹/₂in/ 3.75cm long overall. No other flowering shrub has such an air of the exotic at this time of the year. In the summer, fruit are borne, diminutive bristly golden gooseberries flushing with red. It will benefit from wall protection in the less favoured areas and may be very satisfactorily trained and clipped to shape, but otherwise has no special cultivation needs. The foliage makes an excellent background to other planting, and smaller clematises, for example the summer-flowering *C. viticella*, look very fine trained up it.

Rosa

There are at least 100 species of roses, in the family Rosaceae, widely distributed in the northern hemisphere. There are also immense numbers of cultivars, with novelties flooding from the nurseries every year, but few of enduring garden value. Understandably, many gardeners go mad on roses but they are not particularly easy to use harmoniously in the garden. Large gardens in the past had separate rose gardens which were visited in season and ignored for the rest of the year. Today, in gardens of more modest size, most gardeners have to choose roses to go with the varied seasonal plantings of the mixed border. I have selected a very few, and my main consideration has been that they should be happy partners for other plantings. For this reason I have excluded Hybrid Tea roses, many of which have lovely colours and delicious scents, but none is ornamental when not flowering and the flowers themselves are usually much too big to consort gracefully with other plants. The category of Patio Roses should not be scorned. They are small, rarely exceeding 24in/60cm in height, and many have flowers resembling in miniature the old Shrub Roses, with excellent scent and perpetual-flowering. There is no point in naming names because they are very widely available in varying colours in garden centres. Climbing and Rambling Roses are described on pages 254–56. All roses repay rich feeding, and repeat-flowering kinds should be dead-headed. All are at their best in a sunny position. They may be propagated by cuttings but some of the species will seed themselves in an unaggressive sort of way.

Rosa glauca (R. rubrifolia)
Origin: S. Europe
Height: 8ft/2.5m
Z: 2

❧ This is one of the very few roses whose foliage alone would earn its place in the garden. The foliage is glaucous-grey with rosy undertones, and the new growth is a dusty red, especially marked when seen against the light. The leaves are pinnate, each leaflet 1in/2.5cm long, narrow, pointed and very finely toothed, borne on arching stems. The flowers, in May or June, are single, 1¹/₂in/4cm across, a handsome carmine-pink with a pale eye, and lightly but sweetly scented. This is a wonderfully ornamental plant. It arches gracefully over lower-growing plants and the foliage remains decorative, especially in red and purple arrangements. In late summer the branches are borne down with profuse fruit, at first a rather striking chocolate-brown but turning brilliant scarlet with the cooler autumn weather. It will grow well in part shade as well as in sun, and is very easily propagated by seed or, to perpetuate an especially fine colour, by cuttings.

Rosa 'Iceberg'

Rosa 'Iceberg'
Origin: Garden
Height: 4ft/1.2m
Z: 2

❧ This Floribunda Rose is deservedly very popular. It has rather bold foliage, up to 4in/10cm long, toothed at the margin and a healthy mid-green. The flowers, each 4in/10cm across, double with a creamy centre, start in June and are borne in bunches. Its only weakness is that it has only the vaguest of scents. Otherwise it is an admirable rose for the border, continuing to produce a profusion of flowers very late in the season. There is a climbing version and it is often seen grafted as a standard, which is effective in formal arrangements.

Rosa 'Madame Isaac Pereire'
Origin: Garden
Height: 6ft/1.8m
Z: 5

❧ This old Bourbon Rose, dating from the 19th century, has tremendous character. The flowers in June are wonderful in colour, boldness and scent. They are very double, 6in/15cm across, quartered (that is to say with a pronounced four-part arrangement of petals), and a rich purple-red. They have an extraordinary scent – some say the very best of any rose – very deep and sweet but with a touch of citrus that gives it astringent spice. After the first great flowering there are scatterings of flowers throughout the season. The leaves have a grey metallic hue and are oval, slightly toothed, up to 2in/5cm long. It makes a substantial bush or it may be trained against a wall. At all events it is essential to place it so that the full glory of its perfume may be appreciated.

Rosa 'Madame Isaac Pereire'

Rosa moyesii
Origin: China
Height: 10ft/3m
Z: 5

❦ Few of the great wild roses are easy to accommodate in the tame environment of the average garden. Nonetheless, to keen rose-lovers they offer a special pleasure given by no other plant. This magnificent aristocratic Chinese species throws out long prickly upright but arching stems which bear in June lovely single flowers, variable in colour but in the best an intense blood-red, up to 2¹/₂in/6cm across and lightly scented. These are followed by beautiful hips, elegant and up to 2in/5cm long, a good orange-red. It does not, as many wild roses do, form a great thicket and at the back of a border its great branches will curve out above other plantings. It self-seeds happily.

Rosa 'Souvenir du Docteur Jamain'
Origin: Garden
Height: 8ft/2.5m
Z: 5

❦ Many of the very best roses were bred in the 19th century and this magnificent Hybrid Perpetual is one of them. It has lively green foliage and in June, but intermittently throughout the growing season, dramatic very deep purple-red double flowers 4in/10cm across, with a delicious sweet scent. Few other shrubs have such deep red flowers and it is immensely valuable as an ingredient in a border of hot colours.

Salvia

This is a huge genus of at least 900 species, woody and herbaceous, in the family Labiatae, very widely distributed in every continent. For herbaceous kinds see page 152.

Salvia officinalis
Origin: Mediterranean
Height: 36in/90cm
Z: 5

❧ The evergreen culinary sage has a delicious aromatic scent but is not an exciting garden plant. Some of its cultivars, however, have immensely decorative foliage. The species has rounded, pointed, leathery leaves of a light green, 3in/8cm long, and produces little brilliant blue flowers ¹/₂in/1.25cm long in May or June.
S.o. 'Icterina' has splashes of gold on the foliage, making it seem perpetually dappled with sunlight.
S.o. 'Purpurascens' has wonderful dusty plum-purple-coloured foliage, slightly larger than the type, and goes marvellously well with reds and purples (I grow a very dark red herbaceous potentilla threading through it).

Salvia officinalis 'Tricolor'

S.o. 'Tricolor' has creamy margins to the leaves, some of which are overlaid with red. All these may be pruned in early spring to counteract their tendency to sprawl; though as they flower on previous year's growth there will be no flowers. All need sharp drainage and a sunny position. They may be propagated by cuttings.

Sarcococca

There are about twenty species of sarcococca, in the family Buxaceae, all native to eastern Asia.

Sarcococca hookeriana digyna
Origin: China
Height: 36in/90cm
Z: 6

❧ This is a much more glamorous cousin of box (*Buxus sempervirens*) that has the added attraction of richly scented flowers in mid-winter. It is evergreen, a low-growing suckering shrub with very elegant slender pointed leaves, 3in/8cm long, which give a lively texture to the whole plant. The flowers in winter, insignificant and putty-white, are heavily perfumed, scenting the air on a sunny day most deliciously. This is a very good shrub for the border, taking up little room but giving ornament and structure all the year round. It will do well in full sun or light shade and is effortlessly easy to propagate by root division.

Skimmia

Skimmia japonica
Origin: Japan, Taiwan
Height: 4ft/1.2m
Z: 7

There are four species of skimmia, in the family Rutaceae, all woody plants native to eastern Asia.

❧ This evergreen shrub has several qualities which, together, make it a valuable decorative plant. The leaves are oval, glistening, up to 4in/10cm long. Sweet honey-scented miniature panicles of flowers appear in late March or April when the bush is still bearing the brilliant shining scarlet fruit from the previous year. In a border its compact evergreen growth and shapely form will provide structure, and its shining foliage a good foil to other plantings. It has no particular cultivation needs except that, being dioecious, you must have a male as well as a female plant for berries to be produced. It is difficult to propagate by cuttings but berries germinate well, which explains why there is so much variation between plants of the same species.

Sorbaria

Sorbaria tomentosa
(*S. aitchisonii*)
Origin: Himalaya
Height: 10ft/3m
Z: 7

There are four species of sorbaria, all deciduous woody plants in the family Rosaceae, native to eastern Asia.

❧ The foliage of this large shrub is among the most beautiful of any, and with its ornamental flowers it makes an outstandingly decorative plant. The leaves are pinnate, up to 12in/30cm long, and the leaflets, finely toothed, narrow and crisply veined, are up to 3in/8cm long. They are carried on arching stems whose new growth is tinged with purple and their effect is supremely elegant. The flowers appear in July and are entirely worthy of the beautiful foliage; they are generous frothing plumes, up to 15in/35cm long, of diminutive creamy white flowers which have the scent of old-fashioned soap-suds. It must have moisture-retentive soil in a protected position but will do well in semi-shade. If size is a problem it may be pruned in winter, cutting back and removing old stems, which has the additional advantage of increasing flowering. It may be propagated by cuttings.

Stachyurus

There are ten species of stachyurus, in the family Stachyuraceae, native to eastern Asia.

Stachyurus praecox
Origin: Japan
Height: 10ft/3m
Z: 4

❧ Although the flowers of this shrub appear to be of an oriental delicacy they are tough performers, impervious to icy blasts even though they appear at a particularly vulnerable time of year, in February or March. They hang in pendent chains, 4–5in/10–12.5cm long, composed of pale primrose-coloured cup-shaped flowers, suspended from the branches whose pink-tipped foliage is only just appearing. The leaves are pointed ovals, finely toothed and of a downy texture. It forms an upright open shrub and the wood has a handsomely mottled reddish-brown bark. It has no special cultivation requirements and will perform in light shade or in full sun. It makes a good specimen shrub or can be incorporated in a deep border where its light shade will allow other plantings to flourish below.

Syringa

There are about thirty species of syringa, or lilacs, in the family Oleaceae, from eastern Asia and southern Europe.

Syringa meyeri 'Palibin'
Origin: Garden
Height: 4ft/1.2m
Z: 5

❧ This miniature lilac has much charm. The leaves open in April, rounded, light green, 1in/2.5cm across, on purple new growth. The flowers are borne in sprays at the tips of branches, starting as rosy violet buds but opening in May into diminutive pink stars with a sweet

Illustration opposite:
Syringa 'Madame Antoine Buchner'

heavy scent. It is of compact rounded growth and may be encouraged to grow on a single stem, like a miniature tree. It is an excellent plant for a narrow border, beautiful in flower and, despite its small size, with emphatic structural presence. It likes a sunny site and may be propagated very easily from cuttings.

Syringa meyeri 'Palibin'

Syringa vulgaris
Origin: S. Europe
Height: 18ft/6m
Z: 4

❧ The common lilac *is* common, but many owners of smaller gardens may feel unwilling to give space to a large deciduous shrub whose chief virtue is a wonderful but short-lived display of flowers in April or May. The flowers, generous panicles hanging heavy on the branch, have a unique scent, sweet, languorous and slightly spicy. There are several hundred cultivars in existence, ranging in colour from pure white (such as 'Madame Lemoine'), through various shades of pinkish- or blueish-violet (such as 'Madame Antoine Buchner') to the deepest purple (such as 'Michael Buchner'). The shrub itself varies little. Its habit is open, spreading upwards, and the leaves are heart-shaped, 3in/8cm long, and a lively fresh green. In a very large border it can have spectacular presence. It may be propagated by cuttings.

Teucrium

Teucrium fruticans
Origin: Portugal, Spain
Height: 5ft/1.5m
Z: 7

There are about 300 species of teucrium, in the family Labiatae, both woody and herbaceous, and widely distributed in the warmer temperate regions.

❧ The silvery grey leaves and the pale blue flowers of this deciduous Mediterranean shrub are its best qualities. The leaves are narrow, pointed, up to 3in/8cm long, veined and mid-green above. Both the underside of the leaf and the stems of the new growth are the palest grey, like kid gloves. The flowers are single, pale sky-blue, 3/4in/1.5cm long and veined with deeper blue. The bush tends to grow rather laxly but may be clipped tightly in March – in warmer countries it makes an excellent hedge. If this is done flowering will be delayed until June, but otherwise scatterings of flowers are produced at any time in mild weather. It must have a well-drained sunny position where it looks wonderful with other Mediterranean shrubs – cistuses, artemisias and lavender. It may be propagated by cuttings.

Viburnum

Viburnum carlesii 'Diana'

A genus of about 200 species, in the family Caprifoliaceae, very widely distributed in temperate and subtropical regions. Among them are some of the very finest flowering shrubs.

Viburnum × *burkwoodii*
Origin: Garden
Height: 7ft/2m
Z: 5

❧ An evergreen shrub with fine foliage and a wonderful display of spring flowers. Shining pink buds open in May into white scented flowers held in globe-shaped bunches. The new leaf, a fresh mid-green, stands out against the much darker shining green of the old foliage. It will produce a further scattering of flowers in the autumn. There are various named cultivars but none that adds to the distinction of the type. There is, however, a hybrid with *V. carlesii*, *V.* 'Anne Russell', a deciduous shrub with beautiful peach-pink buds opening to creamy pink flowers in spring, and with the same intense fragrance as *V. carlesii*. It has a more open habit of growth, forming in time a handsome sprawling shape. It should be planted in an open sunny place.

Viburnum 'Anne Russell'

Viburnum carlesii
Origin: Korea
Height: 5ft/1.5m
Z: 5

❧ For the smaller garden this is an outstanding deciduous shrub with attractive foliage, a handsome shape and a dazzling spring display of scented flowers. The flower buds form in the winter and by the beginning of March they sparkle like jewels on the leafless branches, globe-shaped groups of shining deep pink buds. The tiny flowers, white within and pink without, have a piercing scent, sweet but with a spiciness that prevents it from being merely cloying. By now the foliage has also emerged – handsome grey-green pointed oval leaves, 2in/5cm long, with much paler undersides. There are a few cultivars, of which *V.c.* 'Diana' is exceptionally good, with glistening red buds and purple-flushed foliage; although vigorous, it forms a neat and shapely bush. It is an ideal border plant, where its shape gives structure and its distinguished foliage makes a good background to herbaceous plantings. Plant a pair flanking the opening of a path to form a decorative entrance.

Viburnum plicatum
'Mariesii'
Origin: Garden (E. Asia)
Height: 8ft/2.4m
Z: 6

❧ The habit of growth of this deciduous shrub is its most striking feature. It spreads horizontally, giving the impression of being constructed of layers. The leaves are oval, slightly serrated, up to 4in/10cm long. The flowers in May are wonderful – flat mushroom-shaped corymbs of diminutive white flowers carried in profusion along the branches and emphasizing the tabular shape of the plant. The foliage assumes handsome tawny colours in autumn. It will flourish in light shade and is at its best in an informal garden of woodland character. It may be propagated by cuttings.

Weigela

Weigela 'Florida Variegata'
Origin: Garden (Korea)
Height: 8ft/2.4m
Z: 5

There are about ten species of weigela, in the family Caprifoliaceae, all deciduous shrubs from eastern Asia.

❧ The combination of pale pink flowers and cream margined leaves makes this an exceptionally decorative shrub. The leaves are pointed, oval, slightly toothed and up to 3in/8cm long, pale green with wavy cream margins. The flowers in May or June are 1 1/2in/4cm long, trumpet-shaped, deep rosy pink outside and much paler within. Long after the flowers have faded the distinctive foliage colour will continue to decorate the border, where it will be at its best in a sunny position. It should be pruned after flowering to encourage flowering growth, and any branches reverting to the unvariegated type should be removed. It may be propagated by cuttings.

Xanthoceras

There are two species of xanthoceras, in the family Sapindaceae, native to China.

Xanthoceras sorbifolium
Origin: China
Height: 10ft/3m
Z: 6

❧ Fashion in plants is a curious thing and this very beautiful plant has, for no evident reason, become a rarity. It is a superb deciduous shrub with fine pinnate leaves up to 8in/20cm long, each leaflet shapely and finely toothed. It flowers in May, handsome upright white candles, rather like a very refined version of the flowers of a horse chestnut, up to 10in/25cm long. The flowers are followed by curious nut-like fruit. It must have a sunny protected position, and it may be trained against a wall to give protection in cooler gardens. Any pruning must be done after flowering as it flowers on the previous year's growth. It may be propagated by seed or root cuttings.

Yucca

There are about forty species of yucca, woody and herbaceous, in the family Agavaceae, all native to North America and the Caribbean. The species described below are clump-forming and each 'crown' bears only one flower stem and subsequently dies. But flower-bearing crowns may easily be removed and a continuity of flowers ensured from year to year. In the wild they are pollinated by moths and thus their scent is more pronounced in the evening.

Yucca filamentosa
Origin: North America
Height: 6ft/1.8m
Z: 4

❧ The blade-like evergreen foliage and the exquisite summer flowers of this yucca make it an exceptional plant. The leaves, pointed but not dangerously sharp as in some species, grow stiff and upright, up to $2^{1}/_{2}$ft/ 75cm long. The flowers, held in generous heads, are carried on bold fleshy stems. Long before the flowers open the buds handsomely ornament the plant. They point upwards, the calyces giving the whole flower head a pink glow; as the bud begins to open the colour changes to a green-tinged ivory. When fully open the flowers hang gracefully downward, each like a half-open tulip, a marvellous creamy white in colour and up to 2in/5cm long. It has tremendous character in the border or planted as a pair, forming a dramatic and exotic opening to a path or gate. It should be well fed and must have a sunny position and, if possible, one that is protected from violent winds which may damage the tall flower stems.

CLIMBERS
AND
WALL PLANTS

— ❧ —

I have included in this section some plants that
have no natural climbing propensity but which
may benefit from the protection afforded by a
wall. Walls, of course, are far from necessary for
most climbing plants, which may find the support
they need on trellis, posts, arbours, pergolas or,
sometimes most decoratively of all, on other
plants. Some of the plants I have included,
especially the summer-flowering clematis, make
excellent border plants, growing more or less
horizontally and weaving through other
plantings.

There is something irresistibly attractive about
generous swags of climbers festooning a wall.
Although there is a lot of work in the proper
training and pruning of climbing plants, the
decorative rewards are high. An abundantly
flowering climbing rose or clematis, displayed to
great advantage on a vertical support, gives a
dramatic show of flowers that few shrubs can
match. A trellis or wall as a backdrop to a border
adds a pronounced vertical dimension as well as
giving protection to the border. Many different
plants may be accommodated, interweaving
attractively, and perhaps straying decoratively
into the branches of nearby shrubs. This blurs the
crisp division of the horizontal and the vertical,
giving a wonderful feeling of abundance.

Most of the climbers I describe are ornamental
chiefly because of their flowers. Others, ivies and

vines in particular, have practical uses as well; their superb, sometimes evergreen, foliage can be used to conceal some ugly building or to provide shade. Either way, climbers and wall shrubs are essential components of the repertoire of garden plants.

Actinidia

There are about forty species of actinidia, in the family Actinidiaceae, all native to eastern Asia.

Actinidia kolomikta
Origin: E. Asia
Height: 12ft/3.6m
Z: 5

❧ The curious foliage of this deciduous climber is its most decorative feature. The emphatically veined leaves, wide, rounded and pointed, 5in/13cm long, vary in colour. Some are suffused with brownish-red and some, on the male plant only, are splashed with white and tinged with pink, as though dribbled with paint by a careless decorator. It has no special requirements of soil but it does need a sunny position to develop its colouring. It makes an admirable and not excessively vigorous climber for an arbour or archway. It may be propagated by cuttings or by layering.

Akebia

Akebia quinata
Origin: China, Japan,
Korea
Height: 20ft/6m
Z: 5

There are about five species of akebia in the family Lardizabalaceae, all native to eastern Asia.

❧ This strongly twining climber, if kept under control, is an admirable plant. It is evergreen in milder areas and has decorative five-lobed leaves borne on purplish stems. The flowers open in late April from spherical buds; both male and female flowers are carried. The male is rather insignificant, a wishy-washy purple and quite small, but the female flowers are much bigger, 1in/2.5cm across, a deep plummy purple with three-cupped petals (actually sepals) and a marvellous scent – rich, sweet and spiced like the most expensive French soap. I grow it on a wall in a shady corner where it sees little sun. It mingles happily with the rose 'Albertine' whose lavish pink flowers and even sweeter scent take over when the akebia has finished flowering. It has no special needs of soil and is easily propagated by layering. If it threatens to become uncontrollably large – and they become rampant in conditions that suit them – it may be pruned hard after flowering.

Chaenomeles

Chaenomeles japonica
Origin: Japan
Height: 8ft/2.5m
Z: 5

There are three species of chaenomeles, or flowering quince, in the family Rosaceae, all deciduous shrubs native to eastern Asia.

❧ Although a shrub, and with no natural urge to climb, the chaenomeles is often treated as a wall plant, benefiting from the protection to encourage flowering and fruiting. The single flowers, 1½in/4cm across, are at first cup-shaped, then open out, a dashing brownish-red with pronounced yellow anthers. Flowering in March it gives a welcome blast of brilliant colour, a useful change from the predominantly white, blue and yellow of spring bulbs. It produces very decorative quince-like fruit, irregular and golden-yellow, with a sweet and piercing scent; they may be used in cooking in the same way as quinces. Close pruning (taking care of long sharp thorns) in late summer will keep the plant neat and promote flowering. There is a white form,

Chaenomeles japonica

C.j. alba, of dazzling purity, and countless cultivars of hybrids with other species, giving various shades of red, orange and pink; one, *C.j.* 'Apple Blossom', has particularly attractive mottled flowers of pink and white, a lovely spring ornament.

Chimonanthus

Chimonanthus praecox
Origin: China
Height: 10ft/3m
Z: 7

There are six species of chimonanthus, all woody plants in the family Calycanthaceae, native to central and southern Asia.

❧ The wintersweet is a large deciduous shrub which produces in mid-winter the most deliciously scented flowers of almost any flowering plant, like an intensely sweet fruit salad with overtones of very ripe banana. The flowers themselves, borne on leafless stems, make a brilliant winter ornament. They hang downwards, stiff tassles of the palest creamy yellow waxy petals, with warm red interiors. In most gardens it will need the protection of a wall against which it may be trained and where it can catch the winter sun. It should be pruned

hard back after flowering to encourage the formation of flower buds on the new season's growth. The leaves, 6in/15cm long, are oval and pointed and make a boldly textured background for smaller summer-flowering plants. It is easy to propagate from seed or by layering.

Clematis

There are over 200 species of clematis, deciduous and evergreen, in the family Ranunculaceae, widely distributed in every continent in the world. It is hard to imagine any good garden, of whatever size, being without one or more specimens of this most beautiful climbing plant. As a general rule I have found the species much easier and more resistant to disease than the cultivars; however, many of the latter are extremely beautiful and the keen gardener will want to lavish the care on them that they demand. All clematises should have a sunny position but their roots need to be cool and moist; some gardeners put a slab of stone at their base or shade the roots with another plant. A substantial mulch in spring will promote growth and flowering. They may be propagated, often with difficulty, by inter-nodal cuttings, or by seed.

Clematis 'Alba Luxurians'
Origin: Garden
Height: 8ft/2.5m
Z: 5

This has curiously attractive flowers which happily intermingle with other climbing plants. The flowers are grey-white, occasionally tipped with green, 2in/5cm across, with very dark stamens. They hang down, gracefully bell-shaped, but open out fully in the sun. They appear in late June or July and are borne for a very long season. I grow it trailing through *Wisteria sinensis* and the ceanothus 'Gloire de Versailles'. It should be cut down to three or four buds from the ground in the spring.

Clematis chrysocoma sericea

Clematis chrysocoma sericea
Origin: China
Height: 8ft/2.5m
Z: 6

❧ It is the refined detail of this deciduous clematis that bowls you over. The leaves are three-part, elegantly pointed and lobed and suffused with reddish-bronze. The flower buds fatten up in April, globular and fruit-like; they are white but the base is brushed with carmine. The flowers open in late April or May, 2in/5cm wide, single, with ruffled edges, very pale cream with hints of green and lavish lime-green stamens. A second scattering of flowers is also produced in late summer. It is at its best on a sunny wall but will tolerate part shade. It is an excellent climber to ornament the gaunt stems of such climbing roses as 'Albertine'. It flowers on the previous season's growth and therefore should be pruned, if necessary for reasons of space, only after flowering.

Clematis cirrhosa balearica
Origin: Balearic Islands
Height: 12ft/3.6m
Z: 8

❧ This evergreen clematis has fern-like foliage, deeply cut and very elegant, and produces exquisite flowers at a time of year when no other climber can show anything quite so exotic. The flowers, in February or March, are bell-shaped, 2in/5cm long, very pale yellow and freckled with red spots within, and in warm sun have a faint but distinct sweet lemony scent. The new

foliage has fine bronze tints which are also produced by cold weather. This clematis really needs a sunny well-protected wall to perform at its best. It must have deep fertile soil in which it will grow very vigorously but it can be kept under control by pruning hard after flowering.

Clematis 'Comtesse de Bouchaud'
Origin: Garden
Height: 10m/3ft
Z: 6

❧ The mauve-pink flowers of 'Comtesse de Bouchaud' appear in early July after the first period of summer profusion is over. The flowers are single, up to 6in/15cm across, with creamy yellow stamens that look charming with the pink sepals. It is an admirable plant for the usual climbing uses but it is also excellent in the border where it may support itself on shrubs or straggle attractively through herbaceous plantings; I have seen it looking absolutely wonderful straying through a drift of the silver thistle *Eryngium giganteum*. It should be pruned in March down to 24in/60cm above ground.

Clematis 'Countess of Lovelace'
Origin: Garden
Height: 10ft/3m
Z: 6

❧ The spectacular flowers of this splendid cultivar appear in May, vast pom-poms, 6in/15cm across, composed of very many slender sepals of smoky violet-blue. The leaves are striking, heart-shaped and 4in/10cm long. It enjoys a sunny position and lavish feeding and should be pruned hard back in late winter.

The flowers are very big and in any association planting it is important to bear this in mind; in my garden it intermingles with the cream-buff rose 'Gloire de Dijon' and looks wildly romantic.

Clematis 'Etoile Violette'

Clematis 'Etoile Violette'
Origin: Garden
Height: 12ft/3.6m
Z: 6

&❧ This is one of the vigorous but delicate smaller-flowered viticella clematises, flowering on the current season's growth in July. The single flowers are beautiful, rather cupped at first, very dark red-purple changing when fully open to rich blue-purple. The sepals, of which there are between four and six, curve elegantly back at the tips, throwing into prominence the thick tuft of pale yellow stamens. Apart from its striking beauty the value of this clematis is that it will easily put on 10–12ft/3–3.6m in a growing season after it has been pruned to 24in/60cm above the ground in March. I grow it climbing through the branches of *Amelanchier laevis*, in the shade of whose foliage it flowers quite happily.

Clematis 'Gravetye Beauty'
Origin: Garden
Height: 10ft/3m
Z: 6

&❧ This hybrid clematis, one of whose parents is the native Texan *Clematis texensis*, is a brilliant ornament of the late summer garden. Its buds become visible in early July and towards the end of the month each bud sprouts a red point and gradually opens to form a shape that startlingly resembles an airborne tulip. When fully open it reveals its rich velvet crimson colour, with

sepals elegantly curving back, each up to 2in/5cm long,
with a prominent cluster of pale lemon stamens at the
centre. It continues producing flowers for several
weeks. I grow it on an old stone wall and it weaves
vigorously through other planting in the border below,
looking especially beautiful among the pale pink
trumpets of *Abelia × grandiflora* which flowers at the
same time. It must have a sunny position and it should
be pruned to 24in/60cm above the ground in March.

Clematis montana rubens
Origin: Garden (China)
Height: 20ft/6m
Z: 5

❧ This is a very common clematis but quite
uncommon in its beauty: one of the more vigorous,
growing rapidly to its maximum height, it has great
delicacy of flower and leaf. The flowers open in May,
2in/5cm across, four-petalled, dusty pink with
emphatic lime-green stamens, and when flowering in
quantity give off a delicious sweet scent. The new
foliage is very decoratively flushed with bronze-purple
and the leaves are held in threes, each leaflet 1in/2.5cm
long, slender, pointed and slightly lobed. It flowers best

Illustration opposite:
Clematis montana rubens

Clematis viticella
'Purpurea Plena Elegans'

Clematis viticella
'Purpurea Plena Elegans'
Origin: Garden
Height: 10ft/3m
Z: 5

on a sunny wall and will mix to great effect with other plants. I grow in through a large old *Solanum crispum* which flowers at the same time, producing a heady cocktail of scents. Bold gardeners will let it rip; if it needs curbing it should be pruned after flowering.

❧ This exotic clematis has been long in cultivation and is an exceptionally attractive and valuable climber. It starts to flower at the beginning of July and continues for a long period. The flowers are very double, opening gradually from the cluster of sepals at the centre and finally forming a substantial rosette 2$^{1}/_{2}$in/6cm across. In colour they are an excellent rosy purple and the unopened sepals have an elegant silver sheen. It is beautiful on walls or arbours but it may also be used to festoon shrubs such as philadelphus which have flowered earlier in the season. It should be pruned down to 24in/60cm above ground in March.

Eccremocarpus

Eccremocarpus scaber
Origin: Chile
Height: 10ft/3m
Z: 9

There are five species of eccremocarpus, or glory flower, in the family Bignoniaceae, all from South America.

❧ It is the combination of flower, foliage and fruit that makes this vine such an attractive and valuable plant. It is herbaceous and self-supporting. In cooler gardens it will almost invariably be cut down to the ground in the winter but will shoot again or grow from self-sown

seeds. It may also be treated successfully as an annual. The foliage is beautiful, grey-green pinnate leaves up to 2in/5cm long, each leaflet delicately lobed. The flowers, from June onwards throughout the growing season, are little tubes of orange, $^{1}/_{2}$in/1.25cm long, carried in bunches and looking most elegant against the grey leaves. Curious gnarled bladder-like seed-pods with purple-brown calyces are formed, and appear at the same time as new growths of flowers. It must have a sunny position and can most successfully be grown to scramble up a hedge; it looks wonderful against the dark green of yew. It may be propagated by seed.

Hedera

*Hedera algeriensis
(H. canariensis)*
Origin: North Africa
Height: 20ft/6m
Z: 8

There are about ten species of hedera, or ivy, all evergreen climbing plants, in the family Araliaceae, native to North Africa, Asia Minor and Europe.

This North African ivy is only for milder areas. It has bold heart-shaped leaves, up to 4in/10cm long, of an excellent deep glistening green, held on rich red stems which contrast splendidly with the foliage. A cultivar, *H.a.* 'Gloire de Marengo', is sumptuously margined in irregular patterns of cream. It has a marvellous languid air and looks beautiful draped over a low wall like some exotic garment. It will grow in a dry place but it does need protection from cold winds. It may be propagated by cuttings or layerings.

Hedera helix
Origin: Europe
Height: 25ft/7.5m
Z: 5

❧ The common European ivy, seen draping countless trees and ruined buildings, has a lugubrious air, but some of its many cultivars are valuable and attractive garden plants. One of their most precious qualities is that they will flourish in dry shade where their glistening foliage is seen at its most alluring. I find those with deeply cut leaves and long lobes by far the most elegant. Some cultivars are less hardy than the type; the following are all hardy to Zone 7. *H.h.* 'Irish Lace' has very long elegant pointed lobes, up to 4in/10cm long. *H.h.* 'Koniger's' is a warm gold colour with curving blade-like lobes of great elegance. *H.h.* 'Pedata' has glistening rich green leaves with slender pointed lobes of which the central one is the longest, up to 3½in/9cm. It has pronounced pale green veins and is a very quick grower.

Humulus

There are two species of humulus, or hop, in the family Cannabidaceae, both fast-growing twining plants.

Humulus lupulus 'Aureus'

Humulus lupulus 'Aureus'
Origin: Garden (Europe)
Height: 15ft/4.5m
Z: 5

❧ The golden hop, less vigorous than the type, whose beautiful and mysterious flowers are used in brewing, is a vigorous herbaceous climber with dazzling foliage. The leaves are very large, deeply lobed with serrated edges, 5–6in/12.5–15cm across, a warm yellow-green in colour. In the garden it is a marvellous plant for pergolas or trellis, where it may form a valuable summer sun-shade. It looks wonderful intertwined with the deep purple summer-flowering *Clematis viticella* 'Royal Velours'. It likes rich soil, in sun or semi-shade, and may be propagated by division.

Hydrangea

There are about 100 species of hydrangea, in the family Hydrangeaceae, native to Asia and North and South America. Apart from this climbing plant there are some outstanding shrubs; see pages 192–94.

Hydrangea anomala petiolaris
Origin: Japan, Korea and Taiwan
Height: 36ft/10.8m
Z: 5

❧ One of the few entirely self-supporting climbers, this, apart from its great decorative qualities, has the advantage that it will flourish on a north wall. It is deciduous and the first sign of stirring life is the swelling of the leaf buds which are very ornamental,

plump but with pointed ends and of a glistening mahogany colour. The new foliage, in March, is of a fresh mid-green and the flowers emerge from the centre in April, unfolding corymbs of pale cream-green that grow to 6in/15cm across and will persist into April and May, lasting particularly well on a cool north wall. The leaves in autumn turn a fine pale apricot yellow before falling. It may be propagated by cuttings or layering.

Jasminum

Jasminum nudiflorum
Origin: China
Height: 10ft/3m
Z: 6

Jasminum officinale
Origin: Asia Minor, China, Himalaya
Height: 30ft/9m
Z: 7

There are about 200 species of jasmine, all woody, in the family Oleaceae, most of which are native to the tropical and subtropical regions.

In any other period of the year this jasmine would be scarcely outstanding, but it provides one of the best winter displays of flowers of any plant – a profusion of pale primrose-yellow trumpet-shaped flowers, 1in/2.5cm long, carried on leafless branches. The leaves that follow are small and unexciting but they are a fresh mid-green which makes an attractive background to summer-flowering climbing roses and clematises which may intermingle with it. Naturally stiff and twiggy in growth, it is not a climber at all but an excellent wall shrub where, in a sunny place, it will flower in December or January. It may be cut back and shaped after flowering, which will also encourage flowering the following winter. It has no special cultivation needs and may be very easily propagated by layering.

The scent of summer jasmine is one of the very finest garden perfumes, heavy, sweet and of tropical richness. The flowers, diminutive white trumpets, open from pointed buds in June and are borne for several weeks. It is extremely strong-growing and is really at its romantic, free-growing best in a place where there will be no need to curb its vigour. The leaves are not very interesting in form, small and pointed, but are of a good dark colour. Old plants form wonderfully contorted trunks. It must have a sunny protected position and may be propagated by cuttings or layering.

Lonicera

There are about 180 species of Lonicera, all climbing woody plants, in the family Caprifoliaceae, widely distributed in the northern hemisphere. All honeysuckles will perform best in soil that is rich in humus and they will benefit from having a cool position for their roots, possibly shaded by a smaller plant. All may be propagated by cuttings or layering.

Lonicera periclymenum
'Serotina'
Origin: Garden
Height: 12ft/3.6m
Z: 5

❧ The true honeysuckle scent, of an irresistible sugary fragrance, is married in this honeysuckle to flowers of special beauty. Borne on purple new growth and of a rich ruby-red, in upwards facing clusters 2in/5cm across, they start to open in June and are carried for weeks. The petals curve back to reveal interiors at first cream suffused with pink, then turning yellow. The leaves are oval, 1¹/₂in/4cm long, pale green and handsomely marbled. The scent is especially pronounced in the cool of the evening when it will carry great distances across the garden.

Lonicera tragophylla
Origin: China
Height: 15ft/4.5m
Z: 6

❧ Of all the honeysuckles this is one of the most magnificent. The flowers in June are spectacular, up to 4in/10cm across, a wonderful yellow-orange, produced in profuse bunches at the ends of stems. The leaves are up to 4in/10cm long, oval and of a decorative glaucous-green, well set-off by the red berries in late summer. It likes rich moist soil and will flourish in the shade where its colours are at their best; in sun, where it will grow perfectly well, the flowers become paler and more yellow.

Parthenocissus

There are ten species of parthenocissus, all woody vines, in the family Vitaceae, native to North America and Asia.

Parthenocissus henryana
Origin: China
Height: 15ft/4.5m
Z: 7

❧ This vigorous self-supporting vine has exceptionally beautiful foliage. The leaves are palm-shaped, each leaflet up to 2½in/6cm long; some are rounded and slightly toothed and others are more pointed and have more deeply cut lobes. Both have a lovely pattern of silver veining, most strikingly visible in the new foliage which is also suffused with bronze. In autumn the foliage turns a brilliant crimson, the pattern of veins still clearly visible. It is at its best in a shady position, bright sun tending to wash out the

subtle pattern of colour. It will throw out strong new growth, and this may be cut back from time to time in the growing season, to keep it in bounds. It may be propagated by cuttings or layering.

Passiflora

Passiflora caerulea
Origin: S.America
Height: 25ft/7.5m
Z: 8

There are about 500 species of passiflora, or passion flower, in the family Passifloraceae, all woody climbers, native to South America, Asia and Australia.

❧ The intricate flowers of this twining plant are among the most exotic that may be grown outside tropical gardens. Emerging from plump purple-tinged buds, they are white, 3in/8cm across, overlaid with narrow filaments radiating from the centre, whose tips and bases are rich blue-purple. The flowers start in June but will continue in sunny weather well into the autumn; in warmer places decorative golden fruit will follow. The leaves are palm-shaped, up to 4in/10cm across, of a fine glistening green. On a fully-grown plant they hang in bold swathes making a marvellous background to other plants. It needs the protection of a sunny wall, south- or west-facing, and will be evergreen in milder places. To encourage flowering, side shoots should be pruned to a single bud in spring. *P.c.* 'Grandiflora' has larger flowers, up to 6in/15cm across. It may be propagated by cuttings or seed.

Rosa

There are about 150 species of roses, in the family Rosaceae, native to North America, Asia and Europe. Roses are essential garden plants and enthusiasts will want to possess a much wider range than I would have room to describe here. There has been profuse hybridization and selection of cultivars and here I have picked out a few of those I particularly like and which seem to me especially garden worthy. All those mentioned may be propagated by cuttings.

Rosa 'Albertine'
Origin: Garden
Height: 15ft/4.5m
Z: 6

❧ An old and popular rambler, 'Albertine' has one of the greatest scents of any flower – rich, sweet and fortissimo. It has very decorative red-pink buds which fatten up in May, contrasting strikingly in June with the bold profusion of double rose-pink flowers 3in/8cm across. This is one of the best roses for swathing round an archway and is especially beautiful among the chalky blues of ceanothus or clematis. It will flower well in a partly shaded position and it should be pruned, if at all, only after flowering.

Rosa banksiae banksiae
Origin: China
Height: 30ft/9m
Z: 7

❧ The true Banksian rose is a vigorous evergreen thornless climber with fresh mid-green foliage whose new growth is attractively flushed with pink. The flowers appearing in May are semi-double, cupped, ³/₄in/4cm across, white and most beautifully scented with a sweet light perfume. A yellow form, *R. b.*

Rosa banksiae banksiae

'Lutea', has very double flowers, a little earlier than the type, of a wonderful very pale yellow; they sadly have no scent. Both require a sunny wall and careful pruning and training. The flowers appear on old growth and pruning must therefore be carried out immediately after flowering and, later in the season, new growth tied in as horizontally as possible to encourage upright flowering shoots.

Rosa 'Madame Alfred Carrière'
Origin: Garden
Height: 15ft/4.5m
Z: 6

❧ There is a splendid generosity about this lovely Noisette rose with its fortissimo sweet scent. The foliage has hints of grey, and the flowers hang gracefully, up to 4in/10cm across, tinged at first with creamy pink. It will begin flowering in June and continue producing flowers throughout the season until the first frosts. I have grown it with complete success on a north wall where the cool site extended the life of the flowers. It flowers on the current season's growth so pruning may be done in March, which will both stimulate flowering and keep it in control.

Rosa 'New Dawn'

Rosa 'New Dawn'
Origin: Garden
Height: 10ft/3m
Z: 6

❧ This rambler has several outstanding qualities. The leaves are glistening green, rounded, pointed and slightly toothed, 1½in/4cm long. The flowers in June are double, 3in/8cm across, very clear pale pink and most sweetly scented. I grow this very successfully in the rather shady corner of a south-facing yard; the delicate pink can look rather washed out in full sun. It should be pruned in the same way as 'Albertine'.

Rosa 'Zéphirine Drouhin'
Origin: Garden
Height: 10ft/3m
Z: 6

❧ This old climbing Bourbon has many virtues. The flowers in late May or June are marvellous – 4in/10cm across, double, a warm carmine-pink going paler in full sun. They are generously borne, deliciously scented, sweet and musky, and continue for weeks. The new growth is very decorative, slightly glaucous and tinged with red; it is completely without thorns. It has an attractively languid habit of growth. It looks magnificent intertwined with the powder-blue flowers of *Ceanothus* × *delileanus* 'Gloire de Versailles'. It should be pruned in eactly the same way as 'Madame Alfred Carrière'.

Solanum

A vast genus of over 1,500 species in the family Solanaceae, which include many culinary plants (for example aubergine, potato and tomato), very widely distributed in the temperate and warmer regions.

Solanum crispum
'Glasnevin'
Origin: Garden
Height: 12ft/3.6m
Z: 8

❧ This vigorous evergreen shrub shows only vaguely climbing inclinations but benefits from the warmth of a protecting wall to encourage the flowers which are its chief ornament. The leaves are veined and pointed, 2in/5cm long, produced on fleshy rather brittle stems. The flowers, appearing in May as hanging bunches of

intense lilac-blue (a richer colour than the type), open into star shapes, 1in/5cm across, with bright yellow anthers. They give off an intensely sweet scent which is splendidly magnified when the plant is in full flower; the violet cloud of colour is a marvellous sight. Smaller scatterings of flowers continue to be produced throughout the garden season. Climbing plants may happily be grown through it; in my garden it intermingles with the rose 'Albertine' to great effect. It has no special needs of soil but does need plenty of sun. It flowers on new growth and may be pruned to shape in early spring when dead wood should also be cut out. It is easy to propagate by cuttings.

Sophora

There are about fifty species of sophora, all woody plants, in the family Leguminosae, very widely distributed.

Sophora microphylla
Origin: New Zealand
Height: 30ft/9m
Z: 8

&. This is not a climbing plant, forming in its native New Zealand a fine free-standing tree, but in cooler gardens it needs the protection of a wall against which it may be trained. The evergreen leaves are very small, rounded and dark green. The flowers are wonderfully decorative; borne in April or May, they form generous bunches of warm yellow tubes, up to 2in/5cm long. It must have a sunny position so that flowering wood may ripen. It may be propagated by cuttings. The rather twiggy growth makes an excellent climbing frame for July-flowering clematis such as the *C. viticella* cultivars.

Trachelospermum

There are twenty species of trachelospermum, in the family Apocynaceae, native to Asia.

Trachelospermum jasminoïdes
Origin: China
Height: 20ft/6m
Z: 8

&. It is a great puzzle why this beautiful evergreen climber is not more frequently grown. It has gleaming evergreen leaves, oval and pointed, 1½in/4cm long. The flowers in June are creamy white, single, 1in/2.5cm across, with one edge of each petal curved back, making

the flowers resemble an old-fashioned aircraft propeller. They are spectacularly scented – sweet, heavy and languorous, the perfume carrying great distances on a light breeze. It is self-supporting and makes an admirable plant for an arbour or shady tunnel. As it flowers on old stems it should be pruned only just after flowering. Although hardier than often described, it absolutely needs a sunny position. It may be propagated by cuttings or layerings. *T. asiaticum* from Japan and Korea has the reputation of being hardier, and all the charm of its Chinese cousin; the flowers have a touch of yellow to them and it has slightly smaller leaves.

Tropaeolum

Tropaeolum speciosum
Origin: Chile
10ft/3m
Z: 8

There are about eighty species of tropaeolum, in the family Tropaeolaceae, all herbaceous plants native to Central and South America.

❧ The flame nasturtium throws out generous trusses of startling blood-red flowers, preferring cool shade which it richly ornaments. It is a a rhizomatous perennial with very decorative rounded six-part lobed leaves, 2in/5cm across, an attractive glaucous-green. The flowers appear in June in the form of little trumpets, 1½in/4 long, like more delicate versions of those of its cousin, the yellow or orange annual

Illustration opposite:
Vitis coignetiae

nasturtium. It prefers a cool position and plenty of moisture at its roots. It is often seen threading its way across the north side of a yew hedge, against whose deep green it looks magnificent. It may also be allowed to straggle horizontally; I have seen it looking very beautiful in a shady bed of hellebores and Solomon's seal. It may be propagated by division.

Tropaeolum speciosum

Vitis

There are about seventy species of vitis in the family Vitaceae, all native to the temperate regions of the northern hemisphere. All climbing plants, they include the wine grape, *V. vinifera*.

Vitis coignetiae
Origin: Japan, Korea
Height: 20ft/6m
Z: 5

❧ This is one of most attractive and amenable of all climbers and no other has its character. The leaf buds appear in April, plump and red and full of promise, to erupt into wonderful leaves, rounded and slightly lobed and fully 10in/25cm across. It will put on much new growth throughout the summer, throwing out fronds 8–10ft/2.4–3m long, and mingling attractively with other plants. In autumn, with the first cold weather, the foliage explodes into fabulous colours – tawny gold, orange and vermilion – with the veins thrown into prominence. Old wood develops attractively flaking bark and the branches grow at odd angles, giving a

venerable and picturesque appearance. It will grow in any well-drained soil and is quite happy against a north wall, although it will do equally well in full sun. Once the desired framework is established, the previous season's growth may be pruned back in January or February to a convenient bud. In the garden it is a valuable shade plant. In a sunny garden in France I have seen it trained over a light framework to form a shady summer house, with the new growth hanging like curtains to the ground.

Vitis vinifera 'Purpurea'

Vitis vinifera 'Purpurea'
Origin: Garden (Europe)
Height: 8ft/2.5m
Z: 6

❧ This is a very ornamental variety of the wine grapevine. Its new growth, both foliage and shoots, is almost white but the leaves as they age become a dusky russet-purple finally turning to a tawny scarlet before falling. The leaves are handsomely lobed, up to 4in/10cm across, and are both extremely decorative in themselves and mix beautifully with other climbing plants. It will do best on a sunny wall where it will produce bunches of small and very bitter grapes. I have seen it looking marvellous with the rose 'Zéphirine Drouhin' and with summer-flowering *Clematis viticella*. To keep it within bounds and to promote new leaf-bearing shoots it should be pruned back to old wood in the spring. It is easily propagated by cuttings.

Wisteria

Wisteria floribunda
Origin: Japan
Height: 25ft/7.5m
Z: 4

Wisteria sinensis
Origin: China
Height: 25ft/7.5m
Z: 5

There are about ten species of wisteria, all woody climbers, in the family Leguminosae and native to North America and eastern Asia. They are among the most beautiful of all climbing plants, and although they must be allowed plenty of room to display themselves at their best, they are well worth it; if you have room for only one substantial climbing plant the wisteria is unbeatable. Wisterias are at their best on a sunny wall and they should not be fed too liberally. Once a good framework has been established vigorous new shoots should be cut back to 6in/15cm in July, and to three or four buds in December. Germinating the seed, or indeed taking cuttings, is extremely difficult. In any case, seedlings may take twenty years to produce flowers – which may turn out to be of inferior quality.

❧ The long racemes of flowers of this Japanese wisteria provide one of the most dazzling garden sights. In May or June they hang vertically, swaying sinuously in the slightest breeze, up to 24in/60cm long and borne very profusely. Each flower is quite large, up to 1in/2.5cm across, pale lilac and softly scented. There is a beautiful form with especially long racemes (up to 36in/90cm), *W.f.* 'Multijuga', and a good white form, *W. f.* 'Alba'. The pinnate leaves, up to 12in/30cm long, have pale green slightly pointed leaflets.

❧ This Chinese wisteria adds to the beauty of its flower and foliage a wonderfully fresh sweet scent. The buds, large and furry, fatten up on the leafless branches in late March. In April or May they unfold, pale violet-coloured racemes 10in/25cm long, weighed down by the profusion of flowers. The new leaves start to appear at the same time, feathery and elegant, at first flushed with a pale bronze but maturing to a fresh mid-green. They are pinnate, 10in/25cm long, each leaflet rounded, pointed and with undulating margins. The foliage is very beautiful and roses and clematises, for example look marvellous intermingled with it. There is a handsome white form, *W.s.* 'Alba', and some fancy deeper colours no better than the type.

TREES

❧

By trees I mean large woody plants that normally form a single clear trunk with branching growth above. I have limited my choice to smaller trees that may be accommodated in gardens of modest size. A three-hundred-year-old oak set in vast parkland may give the ultimate tree experience, but something of that experience may still be found in younger and smaller trees.

Trees are versatile plants, making a unique contribution to the garden layout, and there are few gardens which cannot find space for at least one tree. A small tree may find a decorative place in the mixed border; a single specimen set in a lawn can impart vivid character to its surroundings. A tree can act as the linch-pin in holding together a group of other large plants. A tree will almost certainly be the largest plant in the garden, its vertical emphasis leading one's eye to the sky and so opening out an otherwise possibly claustrophobic design.

The light canopy of a deciduous tree can give cooling shade on a hot summer's day. It may also provide the right environment for other plants: the natural leaf-mould conditions demanded by many woodland plants, for example.

Trees, to a greater degree than any other plant, convey the seasonality of the passing months. A deciduous tree may be strikingly ornamental in spring when its fresh new leaves are followed by flowers; in summer, fully developed foliage will determine its individual character; in autumn it may have decorative colour or beautiful fruit;

while in winter, when an evergreen will stand proudly alone, the absence of leaves on its deciduous brother may reveal some lovely pattern of branches or colouring of bark. No other plant has such power to introduce into the garden the true spirit of nature.

Acer

There are about 150 species of maples, all woody, in the family Aceraceae, widely distributed in every continent in the northern hemisphere. Unless otherwise indicated, all those described below will do best in part shade in rich moist but well-drained soil. All may be propagated by seed which in most cases is prolifically borne.

Acer campestre
Origin: Europe
Height: 40ft/12m
Z: 6

❧ The European field maple is not a rare tree but it is a handsome one that well merits a place in the garden. The mid-green leaves, 3in/8cm across, have pointed lobes, and new growth is decoratively flushed with pink. In autumn the foliage colours a superb yellow. It forms an upright tree with a rounded crown and in the wild is found in rather light alkaline soil. For the less formal parts of the garden, especially boundaries giving onto countryside, it makes a marvellous hedge with a lively texture; plants should be 18in/45cm apart and the hedge may be loosely clipped in summer.

Acer capillipes
Origin: Japan
Height: 42ft/12m
Z: 5

❧ The snake-bark of this Japanese maple is ornamentally striped, and its colouring subtle and beautiful: fissures of pale green against a deeper background. The new growth starting in April is dramatic; glistening buds open into scarlet shoots bearing the unfolding new foliage, each leaf up to 4in/10cm long, lime-green, broad and shapely with pointed lobes. The seed pods are very ornamental, hanging in generous dangling festoons through the summer. It forms a rather upright pyramid-shaped tree and its autumn foliage is a brilliant russet orange. There is always something to admire in this maple; in deep mid-winter its leafless branches display their striations to best effect.

Acer davidii
Origin: China
Height: 50ft/15m
Z: 6

❧ Another snake-bark maple which has much in common with *Acer capillipes* but the leaves are rounded, dark, glistening green, slightly toothed and up to 6in/15cm long. The bark has pale striations on a pinkish-brown ground. The diminutive yellow flowers in April hang in chains on red stems. The fruit in late summer is very handsome: trusses of winged seed pods, turning pinkish-brown, sway decoratively in the breeze. The autumn foliage is a beautiful orange-red. It varies considerably in habit: some trees in maturity are rounded and broadly spreading, others more upright.

Acer griseum
Origin: China
Height: 30ft/9m
Z: 6

❧ This tree has distinction and beauty in all its parts at any time of year. The foliage opens in April, an ethereal and striking sight, and passes through a dazzling sequence of colours – brown, pink and cream – before assuming a handsome fresh mid-green. The leaves are grouped in threes, each slightly toothed and lobed, 2in/5cm long, resembling an aristrocratic oak leaf. In the autumn it colours brilliantly, a deep red with purple overtones. Finally, the bark is wonderfully ornamental. It peels away from the trunk and branches, a fresh speckled tawny-russet colour, showing the more sombre tones of the wood beneath. It grows slowly to form an upright tree, in time rather rounded, and is

undemanding as to cultivation. Although fruit is prolific, very little will germinate, and it is otherwise hard to propagate. In a woodland clearing or standing alone in a position of prominence it is a wonderful tree.

Acer japonicum aureum

Acer japonicum
Origin: Japan
Height: 30ft/9m
Z: 6

❧ This Japanese maple is very rarely seen in its type, and forms are much more garden worthy. *A. j. aconitifolium* has large deeply lobed and toothed leaves, up to 6in/15cm across, mid-green turning rich carmine in autumn. *A.j. aureum* (now renamed *A. shirasawanum aureum* by some authorities) has striking pink glistening buds which open in April or May, the leaves a vivid lime-green, delicately pleated and contrasting decoratively with the pink outer bud. The leaves are rounded with toothed points, 4in/10cm across, and remain a fresh yellow-green throughout the season. It prefers light shade as the foliage is susceptible to damage by scorching. In time these maples form marvellously elegant spreading open trees, wonderful in woodland to contrast with sturdier trees.

Acer palmatum
Origin: Japan
Height: 25ft/7.5m
Z: 6

Illustration above:*Acer palmatum atropurpureum*
Opposite:
Acer pensylvanicum

ॐ A very variable Japanese maple, this has produced some irresistibly glamorous ornamental forms. The type has leaves like an open hand, up to 4in/10cm across, and each leaflet is delicately toothed and a lively green colour. The fresh young foliage in April is followed by dangling diminutive flowers, insignificant in form but a purple-red in colour, that contrast decoratively with the fresh green leaves. In autumn the foliage colours a brilliant red. It forms a tree of handsome habit, spreading horizontally, with low-growing branches of great delicacy. It will do best in deep rich soil, in sun or semi-shade, and should be protected to the north and east, as very cold wind in the spring can harm the foliage. It may be propagated by seed. *A.p. atropurpureum* is a glowing deep red form. *A.p. dissectum* has feathery fern-like foliage of exquisite delicacy and forms a rounded low tree (up to 10ft/3m). There are red- and purple-leaved cultivars of it. *A.p.* 'Senkaki' has startling coral bark, vivid in new

growth, contrasting brilliantly with lime-green foliage. All these are admirable specimen trees or essential ingredients for a garden of Japanese flavour. But they *are* exotic, and demand a sophisticated setting.

Acer pensylvanicum
Origin: N.E. North America
Height: 42ft/12m
Z: 3

❧ This, the moosewood, is the only North American snake-bark maple and it makes an especially handsome tree. The striations are very elegant, tracings of the palest grey on a grey-green background. The flowers in April are striking dangling tassles of lemon-yellow up to 6in/15cm long, and the foliage is big and decorative – up to 7in/17cm long, rounded with pointed lobes, a lively fresh green. The autumn colour is splendid, a clear butter-yellow. In youth the growth is gawky, throwing out branches at awkward angles, but it settles down to a handsome upright habit with a marked pyramidal shape. In the cultivar *A.p.* 'Erythrocladum' the new season's growth turns a spectacular scarlet in cold winter weather.

Albizia

There are about 150 species of albizias, all woody, in the family Leguminosae, most of which are native to tropical regions.

Albizia julibrissin
Origin: Asia Minor
Height: 30ft/9m
Z: 8

❧ The elegant feathery foliage and striking habit of the silk tree are its great ornamental virtues. The foliage is very late to open in cool gardens, gradually unfolding its airy fronds in May. The leaves are pinnate, up to 9in/23cm long, and each leaflet of 2$^{1}/_{2}$in/6cm is itself made up of even smaller leaflets. The leaf colour is pale green but each leaflet is very finely edged in red, giving the whole tree a bronze glow. The flowers in July or August are curious powder-puffs, 1$^{1}/_{2}$in/4cm across, creamy pink. It forms a fine spreading crown like a giant parasol. A widely seen cultivar, *A.j.* 'Rosea', has much deeper pink flowers and is usefully hardier (Zone 7) than the type.

Amelanchier

There are twenty-five species of amelanchier, all woody, in the family Rosaceae, almost all of which are native to North America.

Amelanchier laevis
Origin: E. North America
Height: 30ft/9m
Z: 4

❧ In a small garden this is one of a select number of ornamental trees of which it could be said: if you have room for only one tree, choose this. It makes an elegant shape – upright but with a billowing crown. It casts only a dappled shade and thus, while giving protection from the sun, it will allow many plants to flourish underneath its canopy. The fattening flower buds, tinged with vermilion, begin to soften the naked branches in March, and at the end of the month, or in April, enrobe the tree in a dazzling display of white, softened by the unfolding leaves, which at first are bronze-pink. The flowers are diminutive but borne in tremendous profusion, held elegantly upwards from the branches. In the summer it will assume its shapely form, and late in the season develop curious purple-black fruit. In late autumn it reveals spectacular leaf colour, a brilliant rusty red. Use it in the garden as a versatile specimen tree or place in a border, well planted underneath; I have crown imperials (*Fritillaria imperialis*) followed in summer by pale pink phlox (*Phlox paniculata*) and the toad-lily *Tricyrtis formosana*. *Amelanchier lamarckii* shares all the virtues of *A. laevis* and is almost identical except that the leaves are less developed at flowering time.

Betula

There are about sixty species of birch, all deciduous trees, in the family Betulaceae, native to the temperate parts of the northern hemisphere.

Betula utilis

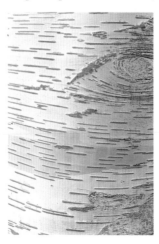

Betula utilis
Origin: Afghanistan,
Himalaya
Height: 60ft/18m
Z: 7

The Himalayan birch has glowing silvery cream bark with coffee-coloured horizontal smudges, an unforgettable colour scheme and a splendid ornament throughout the year; some clones have a much less attractive mottled brown bark. Its habit and foliage are also strikingly beautiful. It is upright in growth but the branches are rather pendulous. Its leaves flutter attractively, causing the tree to bristle with animation; they are rounded, slightly toothed and pointed, up to 3in/8cm long, and their autumn colour is a brilliant yellow. This is a biggish tree for all but large gardens. It is marvellously effective planted as a specimen at the centre of a glade, as is also the form *B.u. jacquemontii* which has dazzling white bark, especially striking on a sunny day in winter. Fastidious owners have been seen on step-ladders with a bucket of soapy water, giving the bark a good scrub to reveal its full splendour.

Carpinus

There are about thirty-five species of hornbeam in the family Carpinaceae, all deciduous woody plants, native to America, Asia and Europe.

Carpinus betulus
Origin: Asia Minor, Europe
Height: 100ft/30m
Z: 5

The common hornbeam eventually grows into a substantial – and very beautiful – tree whose size rules it out as one for any but the largest gardens. But it makes an absolutely wonderful hedge and there is an excellent slightly smaller cultivar. The leaves, up to

4in/10cm long, are oval, pointed and toothed and delicately pleated like a Fortuny dress; new foliage is soft and silky, shimmering in the light, and in maturity a lively green, colouring excellently in autumn to a tawny orange. For hedges it should be planted 24in/60cm apart and clipped in summer. It likes a damp heavy soil and will grow well in semi-shade. A beautiful more compact form is *C.b.* 'Fastigiata' which has a neat pyramidal shape and will not exceed 40ft/11.5m; it is a wonderful tree for a modest avenue or formal walk. A single specimen makes a subtle rounded punctuation mark.

Catalpa

Catalpa bignonioïdes
Origin: S. North America.
Height: 50ft/15m
Z: 5

There are about ten species of catalpa, all deciduous trees, in the family Bignoniaceae, native to North America, eastern Asia and Cuba.

❧ This is an exotic tree of tremendous character. The foliage, which fully unfolds in late April or May, is very ornamental; each leaf is boldly heart-shaped and pointed, up to 10in/25cm long, at first flushed with red and later deep green, veined and with the texture of

flannel. The flowers in July or August are held in airy panicles up to 8in/20cm long; they are splashed with purple and in hot climates are followed by a profusion of long hanging bean pods. It makes a broad noble tree with a handsomely rounded crown. There is a very good gold-leaved cultivar, *C.b.* 'Aurea', which keeps its pale yellow colour throughout the season.

Cercis

There are seven species of cercis, all deciduous, in the family Leguminosae, native to North America, Asia and Europe.

Cercis siliquastrum
Origin: S. Europe
Height: 30ft/9m
Z: 6

The Judas tree makes a very attractive ornamental tree for a variety of reasons. It has an open spreading habit and the leaves, tinged with red at first when they start to unfold in April, are rounded, 4in/10cm across. The flowers appear in May, clusters of shocking pink, often mysteriously erupting from old bark. In autumn the foliage turns a good warm yellow, and in sunny gardens the tree will be festooned with long slender pods whose seed, incidentally, provides the easiest means of propagation. It is said to flower best in full sun. I grow it successfully in a partly shaded courtyard with a pool of *Alchemilla mollis* at its feet. It makes an excellent specimen tree on a lawn. There is a curious white-flowered form, *C.s. albida*, whose new foliage is pale lime-green, immediately followed by startling snow-white blossom.

Clerodendrum

There are about 400 species of clerodendrum, all woody, in the family Verbenaceae and native to the warmer parts of Africa and Asia. Only a few are hardy in temperate climates.

Clerodendrum trichotomum
Origin: China and Japan
Height: 20ft/6m
Z: 7

🍂 Here is a deciduous tree possessed of distinction in all its parts. It forms a rounded rather bushy tree which when old has strikingly gnarled bark and widely spreading branches. The leaves are very fine, up to 7in/18cm long, boldly heart-shaped and of a soft texture and pale green. It August, but continuing for weeks, the flowers open and suffuse the air with their startlingly sweet scent, like lily-of-the-valley out of season. The flowers are carried in broad corymbs, each

bud resembling a maroon bladder and opening into a delicate white star, 1in/2.5cm across. In autumn the fruit continue the decorative interest; they are like bright blue peas and are set off by the rich red calyces that surround them. It is quite sufficiently handsome in habit and foliage to make a free-standing specimen tree. It may be propagated by suckers.

Cornus

There are about forty species of cornus, or dogwood, in the family Cornaceae. Most are deciduous and all are native to the northern hemisphere. Those described below are all deciduous.

Cornus controversa
'Variegata'
Origin: Garden
Height: 25ft/7.5m
Z: 5

❧ This beautiful tree is gracefully harmonious in every detail. Its ornamental season begins in December or January when the leaf buds start to fatten and show a glistening deep red, the colour of old Chinese lacquer. The leaves unfold in April, 3in/8cm long, narrow and curving downwards, mid-green in colour but finely margined in waves of cream. The flowers are carried in flat upward-pointing bunches, 4in/10cm across, creamy white. In habit it presents a tabular arrangement of branches and a marked pyramidal shape. With the light behind it, or with its ethereal foliage emphasized by a dark background, it has unique presence. To ornament a lawn, or as the focal point of some arrangement, there is no more distinguished tree. It is very difficult to propagate and the job is best left to nurserymen who usually graft it.

Cornus kousa chinensis
Origin: China
Height: 30ft/9m
Z: 5

❧ This tree has subtle but irresistible beauty. The leaves, 3in/8cm long, rounded, wavy-margined and pointed, crowd together in stratified clumps, giving the tree distinctive texture. The flowers (really bracts) in May or June are a handsome green-cream at first, 2in/5cm across, held in upward-facing clusters. As they mature they become paler and flushed with pink. It forms a spreading tree, always ornamental, and in autumn the foliage colours brilliantly, a dramatic red suffused with purple. It may be propagated by seed from the curious strawberry-like fruit which need a hot summer to ripen.

Cornus nuttallii
Origin: W. North America
Height: 50ft/15m
Z: 7

❧ The Pacific dogwood has oval slightly pointed leaves up to 5in/12cm long and with the characteristic dogwood curl at the end. The flowers in May, up to 6in/15cm across, are composed of beautiful creamy bracts, usually six in number, surrounding the central button-like deep purple flower. In autumn the foliage turns spectacular colours of red and yellow. Like other dogwoods, this one forms a stately tabular shape. It will be at its best in semi-shade where it may assume a role of importance; except in its autumn colour it is scarcely a showy tree but it exudes distinction.

Crataegus

Determining the number of species in the genus crataegus is a botanist's battleground: there are at least 100, all deciduous, in the family Rosaceae, native to North America, Asia and Europe.

Crataegus laciniata
(C. orientalis)
Origin: S.E. Europe
Height: 20ft/6m
Z: 6

❧ This distinctive and unaccountably rare thorn is perfect for the smaller garden. It grows slowly to form a splendid round-headed tree, with all the character and presence of something much larger. The leaves unfurl in April, deeply cut with pointed lobes, a fine grey-green,

2in/5cm long, like the webbed foot of an exotic bird.
The flowers open in May, 1in/2.5cm across, white,
single, with rounded petals and emphatic dark anthers.
In autumn the fruit are dazzling, glistening scarlet
berries carried in quantity – from which the tree may
easily be propagated. One last decorative feature: as the
tree gets older it develops impressive gnarled grey bark.

Crataegus laevigata

Crataegus laevigata
(*C. oxyacantha*)
Origin: Europe
Height: 25ft/7.5m
Z: 6

❧ Very widely grown in hedges in Europe, this
hawthorn is a very handsome small tree. It puts on its
new leaf in March or April, at first a very fresh pale
green and maturing to a lively shining green. The leaves
are rounded and deeply lobed, 1¹/₂in/4cm across. The
flowers appear in May, very small, single, white,
¹/₂in/1.25cm across, covering the tree and giving off
one of the great spring scents – a languorous,
intoxicating perfume of almonds. The shining scarlet
berries are exceptionally decorative. It forms a
handsome crown, like a large tree but in miniature, and
old specimens have deeply fissured dark bark. It does

well in shade or sun and prefers a heavy soil. It is easy to propagate by seed. There are many cultivars, some of which have rather coarse red flowers, but *C.l.* 'Plena', a very old cultivar, has beautiful double white ones.

Crataegus monogyna
Origin: Europe
Height: 30ft/9m
Z: 5

&. This has much in common with *Crataegus laevigata* but grows bigger, flowers rather later, and has many more thorns. It too will grow into a fine specimen tree but is also outstanding hedging material, especially for country places, when plants should be spaced 18in/45cm apart and clipped in summer. The new growth has a very decorative pink tinge and autumn colouring of tawny red is beautiful. It may be propagated by cuttings or seed.

Cydonia

A genus of a single deciduous species in the family Rosaceae.

Cydonia oblonga
Origin: E. Mediterranean
Height: 25ft/7.5m
Z: 5

&. The common quince is an essential ornamental tree of orchards but it handsomely earns its place in the garden too. Its leaves unfurl in April, rounded, felted and pale on the under sides, 4in/10cm long, hanging rather loose and fluttering attractively in the breeze. The flower buds are pink and plump with a swirling pattern of stripes and the flowers, opening in April or May, are pinkish-white with pink edges to the petals, cupped and facing upwards. The fruit in the autumn is spectacular – like large and irregular pears, a marvellous tawny and yellow colour with an intense sweet and spicy scent. The foliage in autumn colours a warm yellow. A cultivar, *C.o.* 'Vranja', has flowers of a richer pink and much larger fruit. Both need plenty of sunlight to flower and fruit well.

Hoheria

There are five species of hoheria, all woody plants, deciduous and evergreen, in the family Malvaceae and native to New Zealand.

Hoheria glabrata
Origin: New Zealand
Height: 12ft/3.6m
Z: 8

🌿 In the wild this small tree grows up to 30ft/10m but in gardens in cooler temperate regions it will be nothing like so big. The leaves are beautiful – heart-shaped with a delicately jagged edge, suede-soft, pale greyish-green above and much paler beneath, up to 3in/8cm long. The flowers, borne in great profusion, open in late June or July and are single, slightly cupped, white with the palest yellow anthers, $1\frac{1}{2}$/4cm across, smelling faintly of honey. With age it will form a fine spreading canopy but it is not too big to grow in a generous border where it may form a magnificent ornament. The foliage turns a distinguished pale butter-yellow in autumn and is very late to fall. All in all, it is one of the most decorative of all small trees. It must have a protected position in sun or semi-shade and may be propagated by cuttings. *H. lyallii* is scarcely distinguishable, flowering slightly later than *H. glabrata*.

Juniperus

Juniperus communis
'Hibernica'
Origin: Garden
Height: 10ft/3m
Z: 6

There are about fifty species of juniper, in the family Cupressaceae, all coniferous woody plants widely distributed in the northern hemisphere.

❧ The Irish juniper, which has nothing to do with Ireland, makes a very valuable small tree in the garden. The evergreen foliage is grey-green with a hint of blue (but not that oppressive chemical blue found in too many cultivars of conifers). It is slow-growing, with very dense needle-like leaves, and naturally forms a slender upright column no more than

24–36in/60–90cm across. It is excellent planted on either side of a formal walk or repeated rhythmically in a richly planted border to which it brings both structure and a contrasting vertical emphasis. It will not survive water-logged soil but is otherwise very easy to cultivate. It may be propagated by cuttings.

Koelreuteria

Koelreuteria paniculata
Origin: China, Korea
Height: 42ft/12m
Z: 6

There are three species of koelreuteria, in the family Sapindaceae, all native to eastern Asia.

☙ This is a decorative tree of the greatest distinction, producing late season flowers when little else is performing. The leaves start to emerge in late March, unfolding from warm reddish-brown buds which give a glow to the leafless tree. The leaves themselves, at first strikingly flushed with red, are pinnate and toothed, hanging elegantly downwards. The shape of the tree is upright but with a billowing crown. Flowers appear in late summer, plummeting panicles up to 12in/30cm long of golden-yellow pea-like flowers, followed in

warm summers by long trailing seed pods; the seeds are easy to germinate and provide the simplest means of propagation. Finally, in autumn, the foliage turns a wonderful warm yellow, still with tinges of the youthful red. A single specimen of this lovely tree will give tremendous pleasure for much of the year. It may be grown in a large border with other plantings thriving in its light shade; or, best of all, in a position of prominence as a superb ornament in its own right.

Laburnum

Laburnum × watereri
'Vossii'
Origin: Garden
Height: 30ft/9m
Z: 5

There are two species of laburnum, in the family Leguminosae, native to Asia and Europe.

❧ The golden rain tree is a spectacular sight in flower but it also possesses other charms. The leaves unfurl in April, three-part, pale green and softly textured, each leaflet 2in/5cm long and pointed. In late April the flower buds start to ornament the tree, hanging in racemes up to 12in/30cm long, and giving a vertical patterned emphasis to the tree, a waterfall of soft green.

Illustration opposite:
Malus 'Lady Northcliffe'

The flowers, opening in May, a warm but clear yellow, cause the whole tree to glow brilliantly. The brown seed pods (the seeds, and other parts of the tree, are very poisonous) hang decoratively in late summer and the foliage turns a butter-yellow in the autumn. It likes limy soil, will tolerate neutral, and gives of its best in a sunny position. Climbing plants may successfully be grown through it – I have, rather eccentrically, the double white Banksian rose (*Rosa banksiae banksiae*) which flowers simultaneously.

Malus

There are about thirty-five species of malus, in the family Rosaceae, native to North America, Asia and Europe. They include several culinary trees, among them the apple.

Malus floribunda
Origin: Japan
Height: 20ft/6m
Z: 5

❧ The Japanese crab-apple has a slender trunk and rounded bushy crown, giving, in miniature, the handsome appearance of a much larger tree. The flowers are marvellously decorative, borne very profusely (hence the name), appearing simultaneously with the fresh apple-green foliage but almost concealing it. The buds are deep carmine-pink and the

flowers in April, 1in/2.5cm across, open a less deep pink and become paler. It produces very small yellow fruit in autumn. Its good shape and fresh green leaf make it a lovely ornamental tree even when not in flower. It may be propagated by seed.

Malus hupehensis
Origin: China
Height: 30ft/9m
Z: 5

❧ In full flower the Hupeh crab provides one of the most beautiful sights. It forms in its maturity an elegantly spreading tree and in April or May is smothered in blossom; the flower buds are pinkish-white but the flowers open dazzlingly white. The fruit in autumn, reliably prolific, are a rich shining red. It will breed true from seed. It is such a good tree that it should be given a place of prominence in the garden where, unfortunately, it will outface anything less distinguished – a thoroughbred among donkeys.

Malus hupehensis

Malus hybrids
Origin: Garden
Height: 9m/30ft
Z: 5

❧ There are several crab-apples of vague origin that make fine ornamental garden trees. They are very easy to grow but to flower and fruit well they need an open sunny position. All those described below flower in May. 'John Downie' flowers profusely with pink buds opening to white. It has superb fruit in the autumn of a particularly decorative gleaming scarlet, and elongated shape. It has a rather upright habit. 'Golden Hornet' is an old cultivar with pretty cupped white flowers and marvellous tawny yellow fruit hanging on the tree for months and giving it the gleam of gold. It makes a very shapely tree. 'Lady Northcliffe' has superlative pink flowers in May, and ornamental tawny fruit. Old specimens sprawl decoratively.

Prunus 'Shirotae'

Prunus

There are over 400 species of prunus, deciduous and evergreen, in the family Rosaceae, widely distributed in the temperate regions of the world, and including several culinary fruit trees such as the almond, cherry and plum. In spring it is easy to go mad on the Japanese flowering cherries but few are easy to accommodate in the garden and some have very awkward habits of growth. Some (for example *P.* 'Kanzan' with its lurid pink flowers) seem quite overpowering in flower and when not in flower have no distinction of leaf or form. Others (for example the alarmingly fastigiate *P.* 'Amanogawa') are to my taste positively unpleasant. With these reservations, I describe below others in the genus that will give immense pleasure.

Prunus lusitanica
Origin: Portugal, Spain
Height: 45ft/14m
Z: 7

❧ The Portugal laurel is one of those distinguished evergreen trees which, extremely ornamental in themselves, also make a wonderful background to other planting. Furthermore, it has the great advantage that it takes clipping well, and thus is particularly valuable in the smaller garden. The foliage is the great thing – glistening, rich dark green, elegantly pointed leaves up to 6in/15cm long. They slightly resemble the leaves of orange and lemon trees and in colder countries the Portugal laurel was used as a substitute in fashionable 17th-century gardens. The bark and new growth is a fine mahogany brown. It has no special requirements for cultivation and will thrive in semi-shade. In May or June racemes of flowers appear, not dramatically beautiful but with a fine honey scent. Try and choose a specimen with a good tree-like stem – some are of less attractive shrubby growth. A pair, clipped into giant mushroom shapes, make a dramatic entrance, flanking a gate or the start of a path. In a border they may be clipped into structural shapes to add architectural character.

Prunus serrula

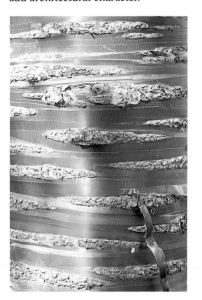

Prunus serrula
Origin: China
Height: 50ft/15m
Z: 5

❧ The bark of this cherry looks like freshly made toffee, a warm red-brown glistening most appetisingly. The old bark peels away and will benefit from a helping hand as it may linger on, turning black and unattractive. The trunk of the leafless tree in winter is a brilliant sight. It forms a rather short-stemmed tree with widely spreading branches and the leaves, up to 4¹/₂in/11cm, are very elegant, narrow, finely toothed, slightly twisted, coming to a long fine point. The flowers in April are small, white and rather insignificant; the fruit in late summer are gleaming scarlet. I have seen this beautiful cherry used to form a short avenue in which the trunks are seen to their full advantage.

Prunus × subhirtella
'Autumnalis Rosea'

Prunus × subhirtella
'Autumnalis'
Origin: Garden (Japan)
Height: 20ft/6m
Z: 5

❧ Few flowering trees perform so reliably in the winter as this attractive cherry, a cheerful sight on a cold day. It will start in November and continue through to the spring, producing blossom at first in scatterings but in greater profusion in warmer weather. The flowers are no more than 1¹/₂in/4cm across, single, pink in bud but opening to white and having a faint but distinct scent of almonds. The leaves are 3in/8cm long,

Prunus × yedoensis

pointed and slightly toothed, yellow-red in autumn. It forms a wide crowned open tree, casting only light shade when in leaf. *P. × s.* 'Autumnalis Rosea' has a lively pink flowers.

Prunus × yedoensis
Origin: Garden
Height: 30ft/9m
Z: 6

❧ This flowering Japanese cherry is a dazzling sight in bloom; it also forms a shape of great character. From a stout trunk, gnarled and black, branches spread almost horizontally, dipping towards the ground. In March or April profuse sprays of loosely cupped white single flowers appear, very slightly washed with pink on the outside, emerging from pinkish-red calyces. The only place for this tree is as a specimen on its own, as a splendid eyecatcher across a lawn where its sprawling oriental character may be fully appreciated. Early spring bulbs – snowdrops and crocuses, for example – will flourish at its foot. It should have a sunny position sheltered from cold winds. *P.* 'Shirotae' is similar in all respects but slightly smaller and with semi-double flowers with a delicious almond scent.

Ptelea

There are about ten species of ptelea, in the family Rutaceae, all native to North and Central America.

Ptelea trifoliata 'Aurea'
Origin: E. North America
Height: 12ft/3.6m
Z: 5

❧ The hop tree in its gold-leaved form is a wonderful small tree. The three-lobed foliage unfolds in April or May, each leaflet up to 5in/13cm long, a marvellously fresh pale yellow at first, modulating to a golden lime-green later in the season, to turn yellow once again before the leaves fall in the autumn. The leaves are held on slender stems which allows them to flutter attractively in any breeze. In June insignificant flowers fill the air with the heady scent of honey. The tree has a particularly attractive habit, slightly sprawling but with a well-rounded crown. I grow it in a partly shaded place against the dark foliage of holly (*Ilex aquifolium*) which shows its pale gold foliage to perfection. It will set seed and this golden form frequently comes true. With its combination of very fine foliage, scented flowers and interesting shape this is an especially good tree for the smaller garden.

Sorbus

There are about 100 species of sorbus, in the family Rosaceae, widely distributed in the northern hemisphere. Among them are some of the very best smaller ornamental trees.

Sorbus aucuparia
Origin: Asia Minor, Europe
Height: 45ft/14m
Z: 2

❧ The common European mountain ash is a good example of a tree which is exceedingly common but never loses its beauty. It has greyish pinnate leaves, finely toothed, up to 9in/23cm long. Flowers appear in May, fluffy corymbs of creamy white, 4in/10cm across. In August it produces some of the earliest decorative berries of any tree, brilliant glistening scarlet or orange against the grey foliage. Its autumn colour is very fine, especially in colder and more exposed areas, varying from biscuit-yellow to superb crimson reds. It is variable in habit from rather upright to rounded and open. A cultivar, *S.a.* 'Beissneri', has an especially upright habit and beautiful pinkish bark; I have seen it beautifully used for a short avenue. It is very easy to propagate from seed but results will be variable.

Sorbus aucuparia

Sorbus cashmiriana
Origin: Himalayas
Height: 20ft/6m
Z: 5

❧ This is unique among the rowans in that it has pink flowers. They appear in May, clusters of very small pink buds opening to single pale pink flowers (which have a curious smell of fish). They are held at the centre of sprays of leaves and contrast with them beautifully. The very delicate rather grey pinnate leaves are 6–8in/15–20cm long, with up to nineteen finely toothed leaflets. Young trees are rather upright but as they grow older they broaden to a more open billowing growth. In autumn the foliage turns a pale

Illustration opposite:
Sorbus cashmiriana

yellow which makes a fine contrast to the brilliant white berries which hang ornamentally throughout the winter. Some plants offered by nurseries are grafted onto mountain ash (*S. aucuparia*) stock; these should be avoided as they will sprout from the base and need cutting back. It makes a supremely elegant and constantly attractive lawn specimen but is not too large to grow in a big border.

Sorbus 'Joseph Rock'
Origin: Uncertain (China?)
Height: 35ft/10.5m
Z: 5

❧ The origin and status of this tree is very uncertain; what is quite certain, however, is that it is a marvellous garden tree. It has a narrow habit of growth with pinnate leaves 6in/15cm long, a good fresh green well set off by the pinkish new growth of the branchlets. The berries vary in colour from cream to sharp yellow and are spectacular with the brilliant purple and crimson autumn foliage. It will not come true from seed and therefore may be propagated only by cuttings.

Sorbus vilmorinii

Sorbus vilmorinii
Origin: China
Height: 25ft/7.5m
Z: 6

❧ This small tree is of the utmost elegance, and even leafless in winter its distinction is apparent. The leaves unfold in April, pinkish-brown, pinnate, very delicate with finely toothed leaflets. The little white flowers in May produce berries in late summer which turn from green to deep pink and to mottled pinkish-white. The autumn colour varies from rich red to tawny. It is rather spreading in habit, with the elegant foliage swaying attractively on lax growth. It is impossible to imagine any gardener regretting planting this exquisite tree. It prefers a deep moist soil and will not tolerate much drought.

Stewartia

There are about ten species of stewartia, deciduous woody plants in the family Theaceae, native to North American and eastern Asia.

Stewartia pseudocamellia
Origin: Japan
Height: 15ft/4.5m
Z: 5

❧ This stewartia, as the name suggests, is remarkably like a deciduous camellia. It is slow-growing and gradually forms a boldly upright tree with splendid oval and pointed leaves, up to 3in/8cm long, which colour a brilliant red in autumn. Creamy white papery flowers, up to 2in/5cm across, with bristling yellow stamens are produced in mid-summer. But the greatest glory of this tree is its wonderful bark – a flaking ochre-orange reveals patches of pistachio-grey. It will do best in a shady position in rich moist soil. It is an ideal tree for the woodland garden but with its handsome shape and beautiful bark makes a very effective specimen on a lawn.

Styrax

A genus of 130 species of trees and shrubs in the family Styracaceae from North America, Asia, Malaysia and Europe. Common names are storax, or snowberry, after the pure white flowers.

Styrax japonica
Origin: China, Japan and Korea
Height: 25ft/7.5m
Zone: 6

ᐳᐦ This small tree is one of the most garden worthy, especially where space is restricted. The leaves, up to 3in/8cm long, are slender, slightly pointed, and have a tendency to grow upwards from the branch, contributing to the elegant appearance of the tree. The flowers, appearing in June, are white, single and shaped like an open bell, hanging in small clusters below the branches. The small fruit, like miniature acorns, are also decorative, hanging well into winter. It is exceptionally graceful in habit, sending out light slightly drooping branches. The foliage, lime-green as it unfolds, preserves an attractive mid-green throughout the season, fading to a warm butter-yellow in autumn. Although prefectly hardy it does best in a sheltered site in neutral to acid soil. In areas suffering from very late frosts flower buds may occasionally be damaged. In the garden it is particularly versatile. Its foliage is not dense so it casts only a light shade, allowing planting underneath. Its white flowers and fresh foliage harmonize well with any scheme. It can be very effective in a border but its roots resent competition from substantial trees or shrubs; bulbs and herbaceous perennials will suit it best. It is also sufficiently shapely and graceful of habit to make an excellent specimen tree on a lawn. It may be propagated by seed or by cuttings.

Taxus

A genus of about five species, all woody, in the family Taxaceae native to North Africa, North America, Asia and Europe.

Taxus baccata
Origin: Europe and
N. Africa
Height: 60ft/18m
Z: 6

❧ In the wild, yew will make a fine substantial spreading tree but in the garden it is usually used for hedging or topiary. The marvellous deep green of the fine needles make yew hedges an admirable background for ornamental planting in borders. The foliage colour varies subtly – the pinkish new spring growth changing to fresh green in early summer and finally to sombre almost black green in autumn and winter. It will grow well in semi-shade or full sun and is not particular as to soil except that it cannot tolerate a water-logged site. For hedging it should be planted at 36in/90cm intervals, and if given plenty of nourishment will easily grow 12in/30cm each year. It needs clipping only once a year, in late summer or early autumn. It may be propagated by seed (which will give a hedge of uneven colouring) or by cuttings.

The Irish yew, *T.b.* 'Fastigiata', is a marvellous plant to give structure in a larger garden; it grows naturally to form a tall billowing column, although it may be clipped to form a more regular shape. A single specimen makes a wonderful eyecatcher and a pair forms a superb frame to a view. There are golden forms of both the common (*T.b.* 'Aurea') and the Irish yew (*T.b.* 'Fastigiata Aurea'), much planted in Victorian gardens and suitable for bold arrangements. A small golden yew, *T.b.* 'Standishii', is perhaps best for smaller gardens, and has an especially good fresh colour. A very handsome cultivar, but needing much space to show its virtues, is the low spreading *T.b.* 'Dovastoniana' which, when mature, makes a splendidly dramatic shape.

Plants for Particular Sites

The following is a list of plants which will flourish in sites of a particular kind. Many plants are extremely adaptable but others will give of their best only in certain conditions; in other circumstances they may survive but they will not flower abundantly and nor will they grow at their most vigorous.

Illustration:
Galanthus nivalis

MOIST SHADE
Allium triquetrum
Arum italicum italicum
Convallaria majalis
Cyclamen hederifolium
Enkianthus campanulatus
Galanthus nivalis
Helleborus argutifolius
　H. orientalis
Meconopsis betonicifolia
Ornithogalum umbellatum
Polygonatum × hybridum
Rosa 'Madame Alfred Carrière'
Stewartia pseudocamellia
Stylophorum diphyllum
Trillium erectum
　T. grandiflorum
Tropaeolum speciosum

DRY SHADE
Asarum europaeum
Asplenium scolopendrium
Brunnera macrophylla
Epilobium angustifolium
　leucanthum
Epimedium grandiflorum
Geranium macrorrhizum
Hedera helix
Helleborus foetidus
Hydrangea anomala petiolaris
Ilex species
Polystichum setiferum
Pulmonaria species
Vitis coignetiae

LIGHT SHADE
Acanthus spinosus
Acer species
Aesculus parviflora
Amelanchier laevis

Anemone × hybrida
Aquilegia vulgaris
Bergenia species
Camellia species
Campanula species
Cornus species
Corylopsis pauciflora
Crocus tommasinianus
Cyclamen coum
　C. repandum
Daphne retusa
Elaeagnus commutata
Eranthis hyemalis
Erythronium dens-canis
　E. tuolumnense
　E. 'White Beauty'
Fritillaria imperialis
　F. meleagris
Galanthus nivalis
Hemerocallis species
Hosta species
Iris douglasiana

Itea ilicifolia
Kirengeshoma palmata
Lamium orvala
Leucojum aestivum
   L. vernum
Ligularia species
Lonicera tragophylla
Lysimachia ephemerum
Mahonia × media
Matteuccia struthiopteris
Nectaroscordum siculum
Parthenocissus henryana
Pieris species
Primula species
Ptelea trifoliata 'Aurea'
Sanguinaria canadensis
Scilla siberica
Smilacina racemosa
Sorbaria tomentosa
Syringa vulgaris
Thalictrum species
Tricyrtis formosana
Tulipa species
Uvularia grandiflora
Viburnum plicatum 'Mariesii'

SUNNY AND DRY
Abelia species
Albizia julibrissin
Alstroemeria pulchella
Artemisia arborescens
   A. ludoviciana latiloba
Asphodeline lutea
Caryopteris × clandonensis
Centranthus ruber
Cercis siliquastrum
Cheiranthus cheiri
Cistus species
Convolvulus althaeoïdes
   C. cneorum
Crinum × powellii
Crocosmia 'Citronella'
Cytisus battandieri
Delphinium tatsienense
Dianthus cultivars
Diascia rigescens
Dorycnium hirsutum
Eryngium alpinum
   E. giganteum
Euphorbia myrsinites
Fritillaria persica 'Adiyaman'

Convolvulus cneorum

Gaura lindheimeri
Gladiolus communis
Glaucium flavum
Iris unguicularis
Jasminum officinale
Kniphofia species
Lavandula species
Lilium candidum
Linum perenne
Myrtus communis
Narcissus triandrus
Nerine bowdenii
Oenothera missouriensis
Omphalodes cappodocica
Passiflora caerulea
Perovskia species
Phlomis species
Phygelius species
Potentilla fruticosa
Pulsatilla vulgaris
Salvia officinalis
Sophora microphylla
Teucrium fruticans
Trachelospermum jasminoïdes

Tristagma uniflorum
Triteleia laxa
Tulipa species
Zephyranthes candida

SUNNY IN RICH SOIL
Abutilon vitifolium
Acanthus hirsutus
Achillea clypeolata
Agapanthus species
Aquilegia canadensis
Aster × frikartii 'Mönch'
    A. novi-belgii
Astrantia major
Briza media
Buddleja colvilei
    B. crispa
Bupleurum fruticosum
Campanula species
Carpenteria californica
Ceanothus species
Centaurea 'Pulchra Major'
Choisya ternata
Clematis species

Penstemon 'Port Wine'

Convolvulus sabatius
Coreopsis lanceolata
Daphne odora
Delphinium species
Deutzia species
Drimys winteri
Eremurus robustus
Escallonia 'Iveyi'
Fritillaria imperialis
   F. meleagris
Galtonia candicans
Garrya elliptica
Gillenia trifoliata
Helenium 'Moerheim Beauty'
Inula magnifica

Lavatera 'Barnsley'
Lilium pardalinum
Lonicera species
Lysimachia clethroïdes
Magnolia species
Melianthus major
Narcissus species
Paeonia species
Penstemon species
Philadelphus species
Potentilla atrosanguinea
   P. nepalensis
Ribes speciosum
Rosa species
Sarcococca hookeriana digyna
Salvia uliginosa
Scabiosa caucasica
Scilla mischtschenkoana
Sternbergia lutea
Syringa meyeri 'Palibin'
Veronicastrum virginicum
Viburnum × *burkwoodii*
   V. carlesii
Weigela 'Florida Variegata'
Wisteria species
Xanthoceras sorbifolium
Yucca filamentosa

VERY MOIST SOIL (Water's edge)
Gunnera manicata
Iris sibirica
Lyschition species

Bulbs

GENERAL
John E. Bryan, *Bulbs* (Two volumes, 1989)
Martyn Rix and Roger Phillips, *The Bulb Book* (1981)

ALLIUMS
Dilys Davies, *Alliums: the Ornamental Onions* (1992)

CROCUS
B. Mathew, *The Crocus* (1982)

CYCLAMEN
Christopher Grey-Wilson, *The Genus Cyclamen* (1988)
Gay Nightingale, *Growing Cyclamen* (1982)

DAYLILIES
Walter Erhardt, *Hemerocallis* (1992)

IRIS
W.R.Dykes, *The Genus Iris* (1913)
Fritz Kohlein, *The Iris* (1987)
Brian Mathew, *The Iris* (2nd edition, 1989)

LILIES
Michael Jefferson-Brown, *The Lily* (1988)

NARCISSUS
Don Barnes, *Daffodils* (1987)
Christopher Grey-Wilson, *The Genus Cyclamen* (1988)
Michael Jefferson-Brown, *Narcissus* (1991)

Herbaceous Perennials

GENERAL
Leo Jellitto and Wilhelm Schacht, *Hardy Herbaceous Perennials* (Two volumes, 1990)
Roger Phillips and Martyn Rix, *Perennials* (Two volumes, 1991/92)
Graham Stuart Thomas, *Perennial Garden Plants* (3rd Edition, 1990)

CAMPANULAS
P.Lewis and M.Lynch, *Campanulas* (1989)

DAPHNE
C.D. Brickell and B.Mathew, *Daphne* (1976)

FERNS
David Jones, *Encyclopaedia of Ferns* (1987)
R. Kaye, *Hardy Ferns* (1968)
John Kelly, *Ferns in your Garden* (1991)
Andrew MacHugh, *The Cultivation of Ferns* (1992)

GERANIUMS
Peter Yeo, *Hardy Geraniums* (1985)

GRASSES
Roger Grounds, *Ornamental Grasses* (1979)

HELLEBORES
B. Mathew, *Hellebores* (1989)

HOSTAS
Diana Grenfell, *Hosta* (1990)
Giboshi Zoku, *The Genus Hosta* (1992)

PINKS
F. C. Smith, A *Plantsman's Guide to Carnations and Pinks* (1990)
PRIMULAS
W.R. Hecker, *Auriculas and Primulas* (1971)
T.J. Wemyss-Cooke, *Primulas Old and New* (1986)

VIOLAS
R.E. Coombs, *Violets* (1981)
R. Fuller *Pansies, Violas and Violettas* (1990)

Climbers

GENERAL
Jane Taylor, *Climbing Plants* (1987)

CLEMATIS
Jim Fisk, *Clematis, the Queen of Climbers* (1989)
Barrie Fretwell, *Clematis* (1989)
C.Lloyd and T.H.Bennett, *Clematis* (1989)

IVY
Peter Q.Rose, *Ivies* (1980)
Jane Fearnley-Whittingstall, *Ivies* (1992)

PASSION FLOWERS
J. Vanderplank, *Passion Flowers* (1991)

ROSES
Graham Stuart Thomas, *Climbing Roses Old and New* (1978)

Trees and Shrubs

GENERAL
W.J.Bean, *Trees and Shrubs Hardy in the British Isles* (Four volumes, 1970-80; supplement, 1988)
D.M. van Gelderen and R.P. van Hoey Smith, *Conifers* (2nd edition, 1989)
Gerd Krüssmann, *Manual of Cultivated Broad-leaved Trees and Shrubs* (Three volumes, 1984-86)
Gerd Krüssmann, *Manual of Cultivated Conifers* (1972)
Alan Mitchell, *The Trees of Britain and Northern Europe* (1982)
Roger Phillips and Martyn Rix, *Shrubs* (1987)

Alfred Rehder, *Manual of Cultivated Trees and Shrubs Hardy in North America* (1927)
Graham Stuart Thomas, *Ornamental Shrubs, Climbers and Bamboos* (1992)

HYDRANGEAS
M. Haworth-Booth, *The Hydrangeas* (1975)

LILACS
Fr. John L. Fiala, *Lilacs: The Genus Syringa* (1988)

MAGNOLIAS
N.G. Treseder, *Magnolias* (1978)

MAPLES
J.D.Vertrees, *Japanese Maples* (1978)

PEONIES
M. Haworth-Booth, *The Moutan or Tree Peony* (1963)

RHODODENDRONS
Peter Cox, *Dwarf Rhododendrons* (1973)
Peter Cox, *The Larger Species Rhododendrons* (1973)
Peter and Kenneth Cox, *Cox's Guide to Choosing Rhododendrons* (1992)

F.C.Galle, *Azaleas* (1987)
D.M. van Gelderen and J.R.P. van Hoey Smith, *Rhododendrons* (1992)

ROSES
Peter Beales, *Roses* (1992)
Michael Gibson, *Growing Roses for Small Gardens* (1991)
Roger Phillips and Martyn Rix, *Roses* (1988)
Graham Stuart Thomas, *The Old Shrub Roses* (1953)
Graham Stuart Thomas, *Shrub Roses of Today* (1962)

Hardiness Zones

Temperature Ranges		
F	Zone	C
below −50	1	below −45
−50 to −40	2	−45 to −40
−40 to −30	3	−40 to −34
−30 to −20	4	−34 to −29
−20 to −10	5	−29 to −23
−10 to 0	6	−23 to −17
0 to 10	7	−17 to −12
10 to 20	8	−12 to −7
20 to 30	9	−7 to −1
30 to 40	10	−1 to 5

Hardiness zones are based on the average annual minimum temperature in different areas, graded from Zone 1, the coldest, to Zone 10, the warmest; thus, if a plant has the rating Zone 7 it will not dependably survive in a zone of a lower number. But the data are only broadly relevant and are more valid for continental climates than for maritime ones. In Britain and many parts of Europe, for example, local microclimate rather than the hardiness zone band is more likely to determine a plant's hardiness. It should also be said that a plant's chances of survival may be influenced by other things than temperature; drainage, rain, amount of sunshine and protection from winds may make a fundamental difference.

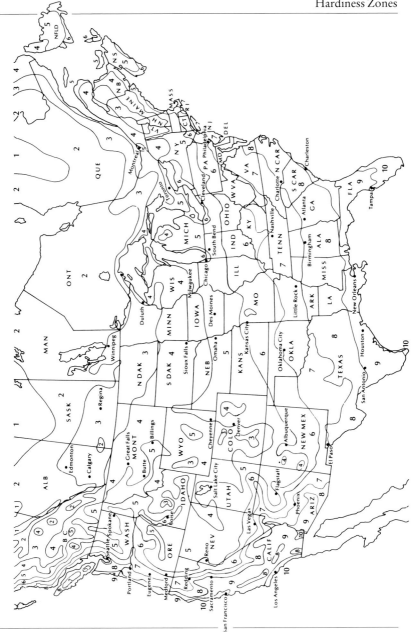